Occupational Treatment

Taylor Brady

atelos

Portions of this book have appeared or are forthcoming, often in quite different form, in *Ambit, Combo, Disaster, Fourteen Hills, Kenning, Mirage #4/Period(ical), plan b, Ribot, War & Peace, Zazil,* the anthology *Biting the Error: Forty Writers Explore Narrative* (Coach House Press, 2004), the chapbooks *Three Poems* (Quinella Press, 1998), *Production Notes for Occupation: Location Scouting* (Duration Press e-book, 2002), *Untitled* (split chapbook with Tyrone Williams, A Rest Press, 2003), and *Mixed-Use* (No Press, 2004), the catalog for Elliot Anderson's CAMS show (Gallery 16, San Francisco, 2004), and the book *Microclimates* (Krupskaya, 2001). Thanks to Christophe Casamassima, kari edwards, Mike Magee, Jason Snyder, Patrick Durgin, Dodie Bellamy, Kevin Killian, Dolores Dorantes, Paul Vangelisti, Leslie Scalapino, Bill Marsh, Bob Gluck, Camille Roy, Gail Scott, Darren Werschler-Henry, Nicholas Laudadio, Jerrold Shiroma, Patrick Masterson, Ryan Murphy, Elliot Anderson, Jocelyn Saidenberg, Dan Farrell, Norma Cole, and Marcus Civin for their support. Thanks as well to Geoffrey Dyer, David Hadbawnik, Tanya Hollis, Sianne Ngai, and Eleni Stecopoulos, who performed a shorter version of "All the Thing You Are" in the 2003 Small Press Traffic Poets' Theater Festival.

© 2006 by Taylor Brady
ISBN: 1-891190-22-9

First edition, first printing

Ŧ Atelos
A Project of Hip's Road
Editors: Lyn Hejinian & Travis Ortiz
Text Design and Typesetting: Travis Ortiz
Cover Design: Travis Ortiz
Cover Photograph, "Untitled" (2004) from Hotel Series, by
    Melissa Dyne. Used by permission of the artist.

Occupational Treatment

> A city is merely a relocation of metals in a certain place.
> —William Carlos Williams,
> *The Descent of Winter*

***

> All these treasures were acquired in a manner that has no future.
> —Walter Benjamin,
> *Moscow Diary*

***

> Does any one separate themselves from the land so they can see it?
> —Gertrude Stein,
> *Narration*

***

> What is the Citie but the People? True, the People are the Citie.
> —William Shakespeare,
> *Coriolanus*

***

> Everything we learned in the suburb has turned out to be true. In adulthood also we will be watched and corrected by our neighbors, whose own privacies will remain impenetrable. We will strive for clarity and order. We will want flowers and the evening return of pleasantries. We will commute between our desire and our economy. Our little fort will be discovered. We will leave.
> —Lisa Robertson,
> "Pure Surface"

Contents

Without Examining the Same 13

Interior Design 17

Apostrophe S 61

Survey Markers 93

Production Notes for Occupation 117

Zoning 179

Without Examining the Same

That Greatest and Worst Of

Here is the catalogue of construction disasters I promised
   works the whole series of enigmas letters each stanza.
Rubbing strangers to pick up a modern smell.

No, the opposite course
               is yet another starvation's craft aesthetic.
"Seeing that nowadays there is product,"
   or mended that imitated perfection
      this facial tic for your amusement
  thereby becoming property
               press 10,000 units of inertia.
– is, beside the works,

     although not wealthy grow hair like
           the point where kink turns task:
   resort is only in themselves
    and windowless, doorless, had been recognizable as such,
    nothing in my mouth so much you.
    Who'd expect ingratitude toward a landing force?
       After so light

water your plot becomes a scheme
was plenty of ground between them —
  own the car in which will die
    such things to help remember

Interior Design

All the Thing You Are

So the opening sequence is a little on the stagy side. Not much camera movement, and the actors are pretty much just talking heads at this point. I might be hoping too much, but I think the FX stuff with the mirror and the sound design for all the voices will maintain enough focus until the real action starts...

We open on a small, tiled bathroom. Camera is stationary, focus wide enough to take in OCCUPANT, who sits to the left on the closed toilet, a door slightly ajar to the right, a mirror over the sink between door and toilet, and a portable radio on the floor to OCCUPANT'S left. Some ambient sound, possibly voices at a party, drifts in through the door. Reflection in mirror slowly dissolves to three PLAYERS, seated in a semicircle around a card table, all facing camera. OCCUPANT begins to fiddle with the tuning dial on the radio.

RADIO:
I connote just what you mark
my word my will would
run. *They flee from me,* their flight
forms me into two, and then a third
stands next to me. Then count it
up, what fell down, pack it in and go.

Fade sound to static, then to background noise. When PLAYERS speak, they seem to read from the playing cards in their hands.

FIRST PLAYER: Do you not think that the owner also suffers loss from an explosion?

SECOND PLAYER: That's why we've created our new weather.

THIRD PLAYER: Hang the tropics. It's summer after all.

SECOND PLAYER: Is there not generally a very great draught every time you open a door or close it?

FIRST PLAYER: But…is this a merely speculative objection?

SECOND PLAYER: That is your name, because you live there.

OCCUPANT tunes in a new station, which momentarily drowns out the PLAYERS, who continue to speak visibly but inaudibly.

RADIO:
They all do, except for him
or expecting him to say
anything. Maybe talking

maybe afraid to ask back
in the grimy part of the closet.
Fullness. Fullness often but
inadequately felt…

SECOND PLAYER: There is a peculiarity of dress?

THIRD PLAYER: Hidden buttons back a clean navy.

FIRST PLAYER: An impressive amount of storage space for sham.

THIRD PLAYER: You are then against education?

FIRST PLAYER: An impressive amount of storage space. That's the best I'll offer. *[slaps the table firmly]*

SECOND PLAYER: I'll take two on margin.

FIRST PLAYER hands a card to SECOND PLAYER.

OCCUPANT reaches down and tunes in a new station.

RADIO:
There they cooled and softened. Cool
and hard. Had he not done his being
clownlike, could they look in speechless
alarm?

> "Who's your organizer?"
> "Which town wouldn't they
> alibi for 'im?"

SECOND PLAYER: Why; is he a marked man for having complained?

FIRST PLAYER: The message board.

THIRD PLAYER: Or just random thoughts. Keep everybody in just enough letters and numbers to say anything you like.

RADIO:

> So it's rather bitter
> it's enough it's smiling

 enough

upstairs you'd say anything right
about then you'd be right about

a brain at work
on getting down
the stairs, fast,

fast surrendering its secret,
this life.
    "Right here! *What
am I looking at?*" Bigger's
the muscle twitched than
limb that wants to move...

THIRD PLAYER: ...or like anything you say. *[triumphantly lays card in front of FIRST PLAYER]*

OCCUPANT *looks up, directly into camera, and sings the touch tones of a seven-digit phone number. PLAYERS pause a few beats.*

THIRD PLAYER: She woke slowly, and with great difficulty...

RADIO:
...to a lurid slashing lance of ambush which then
stopped, falling, hurtling

of bodies there was
a shortage, swung out
from the ceiling

confessed
the question

FIRST PLAYER: *[looking out of mirror frame toward radio, noticing the interruption]* Her head came off the line equipped with holes for air, but no mechanism to cycle the flow.

THIRD PLAYER: That might not be true. What do you know?

FIRST PLAYER: [quick look at radio, which stays silent] A place. A thing or two. In various permutations those make a world of opportunities, or opportunity costs. Intensifying and expanding geographical scale. But nothing got through to her territory…

RADIO:
Four floors of bodies there going back
to the inquest, his sight, clear
sheet of white faces. Standing square
as always, tilted trust upward,
to you. Drinking down
four floors of minor slump.

THIRD PLAYER: …and so she was skimmed off the top. Or boiled down. Reduced to breathless mouthing of the name of her dream…

SECOND PLAYER holds up card received in first deal.

RADIO AND SECOND PLAYER, simultaneously:

…something nasty in a can!

OCCUPANT: It's the usual high-angle shot, pinning me to the floor hunkered down in the bottom left corner of the frame, commanding me to eat.

OCCUPANT turns the dial again.

RADIO [recognizably distinct voices, perhaps a radio play]:
"Yes."
   "And you were…?"
      "Yes,

it was *the tops.*" "*Topos*
of all the maps we draw,

intelligible law and process flow from such condition:
understand them, seek to change their horror or surprise
into honest hate and crime. This is life, the gang's all here."
"The air's all gone. Look at all these questions
                no one ever asked."

FIRST PLAYER: We do enjoy ourselves so.

SECOND PLAYER: Or at least we eat.

THIRD PLAYER: With nowhere to go, the contents made a hole in her face.

RADIO [*new voice, the earnest, rich baritone of a professional radio announcer*]: Later that same day…

[*character actor's voice*] Water is flowing over the walls, and the submerged library is silent on the matter. This is summer humidity or weeping, and just now someone was dead, or else *more real than myself.* Whole histories were failing to happen. The automatic tone arm on Pop's record player likewise malfunctions, returning over and over again to the opening fanfare when it should have ended with a soft return to its cradle, holding me in stasis here in the synthetic-upholstered armchair, muffled in the bulky headphones, when it should have prompted me to lift those padded cups from my head and hear the voices returning to, or retuning, the turbulent indoor air.

The reserve of atmosphere held against my ears is rich with echoes as an empty conch shell, recalling a dream I often have in which I fall off a looming concrete-and-stucco retaining wall through a vast, resonant space, only to land in bright sunlight on the lawn behind the poured slab of a back porch on which my dear dead Auntie Terrible is up to her elbows in some work whose smell erased my brain and shook my convictions long before the dream began. If I might use this occasion to let a secret slip, it would be that horizontal slide, like a roll of utility plastic spread along the grass and sprayed down with a garden hose, along which one's body effortlessly planes before tumbling, scraped and bleeding a little, through the grass and dirt, the rocks and sandspurs, at the far end, by which a day of Auntie Terrible's drowned life itself comes washing in behind one's shallow wake, fluids shared out of season taking form on the solid ground of an encounter that has not yet given up its happening.

OCCUPANT: I did it. I added it. I counted it among my treasures…

Enter INTRUDER through the door to the right, wearing a long shapeless gown or tunic that trails on the floor. INTRUDER pauses briefly in front of the mirror to wink at the PLAYERS, then takes up position leaning on sink between mirror and OCCUPANT.

INTRUDER: Occupied. Be out in a minute.

OCCUPANT: No, you've got it all wrong. You're out of order.

INTRUDER: Yes. Closed for maintenance. Please visit us again.

OCCUPANT begins fiddling with radio dial, rapidly switching from station to station.

RADIO:
…rose from his white man's catalog determined…

SECOND PLAYER: But you are not quite satisfied with the state of morality in the factories?

THIRD PLAYER: A cascade of glass drops shimmers at the tips of our more casual occasions. Six-foot chain included.

FIRST PLAYER: Makes an excellent choice for the family's telescoping base. But would not the opinion of the workman depend upon the poverty of the workman's family?

RADIO:
Outta sight! Saturday evening
and no misery to view the little
feelings. Determined all at home,
the seminal sick exam I
heard is wholesome, unexpec-
ted. Gone secret, discrete
persuaders bloom to be
and break to weeks' defraud,
made smaller inch discussed
in preference to all…

THIRD PLAYER: …from the wall-mounted base to the imagination. Or add architectural detail to the flat eye of retreat.

SECOND PLAYER: Have the workmen confidence in the proceedings at those inquests when accidents occur?

INTRUDER: Is something happening? What is this?

FIRST PLAYER: Machine washable flag, the familiar design officially adopted by the frayed, dyed, and blind.

OCCUPANT: A party. I hate parties.

INTRUDER: "Iron discipline will be required. Questions of organization cannot be…"

OCCUPANT: Are you quoting?

INTRUDER: No. This is not a bill. This is an estimate for budgetary purposes. We should strive to express the conscious will of the…

OCCUPANT: Sshhhh! Something's coming!

FIRST PLAYER: Create a romantic corner for a stain.

SECOND PLAYER: In a room full of rectangles…

THIRD PLAYER: …nondirectional letters become inspiration when they spell a word!

FIRST PLAYER slaps a card onto the table in front of THIRD PLAYER as the line finishes.

SECOND PLAYER: Place an order. Make the call.

THIRD PLAYER: There's something on my line.

OCCUPANT gets up, turns around and flips up the toilet lid. Kneels down, rummages around in the bowl. Camera zooms in on radio, with just the toe of OCCUPANT'S shoe edging into the frame.

RADIO [sung. OCCUPANT begins to hum along with the occasional phrase]:
…a great collation of sucking
sounds for the kneeling culprit.
Prison pledges the offense
well before the grave
accent marking out my side
this side of a distress beyond

the constant, earnest prayer.
I am very right thus to intrude,
sincere toward religion as I eat.

One bird in hand, one
brought down on
the remote. What's left
will be the troubled top,
monkeying the theme
I know is more
and more to take as

leased expanse — not Peace —
as feet, a foreign landscape.
I'll take you out, if ordered.
This was how we spoke about
the weather, like an Nth World
all askew I knew you knew

in stranger slang, perhaps
encroaching, fatherly, "These
are mine." Export flowers stand
still to be revered, as the fairy
children wildly fly apart.

Focus pulls back. OCCUPANT surfaces, turns to INTRUDER with a pair of sunglasses.

OCCUPANT: Here, I made something for you.

INTRUDER: What is its name?

OCCUPANT: It's a football. *[handing over the glasses, which INTRUDER begins to fondle avidly]*. Be careful — it's very powerful. You must not let it leave your grasp.

INTRUDER: *[putting glasses on]* Ouch! It hit my face. I do not excel at this game.

OCCUPANT: Hmmmmmm. No, that wasn't it.

Throughout what follows, INTRUDER is adjusting glasses, taking them off and putting them on again, tasting them, smelling them, etc. OCCUPANT tunes radio to another station.

RADIO:

I was with you going out from dentals,
wandered staring back across
the palate. It is dry,
a desert. Full of dust. Here is water.
Swallow, move the mouth. Blink.

THIRD PLAYER: We did it. We counted it among our treasures.

FIRST PLAYER: Or, as if it were a bead on a long string of like beads, we hurriedly tongued the blood from its reflective surface and did our duty by it.

THIRD PLAYER: We were confirmed in our correctness by a matching gesture playing across it, as if it were a screen.

Tracking shot onto face of radio, through whose speaker the PLAYERS begin singing:

SECOND PLAYER [singing]: Hello stranger…

FIRST PLAYER [singing]: …put your lovin' hand in mine.

SECOND PLAYER [singing]: Hello stranger…

FIRST PLAYER [singing]: …put your lovin' hand in mine.

THIRD PLAYER [singing]: You are a stranger…

ALL PLAYERS [singing]: …and you're a pal of mine.

RADIO: [announcer] Later that same day…

[actor] The monochrome of the little television set shifted what it meant by saturation from black to red, and summer snow fell like milk on blood. Or petals fell on beach sand like the name of a departure…

Cut back to shot of whole bathroom, as before.

SECOND PLAYER: Sealed thus, it will keep, in some back room or other, until we can come to see ourselves believing in it.

THIRD PLAYER: Ummmm…yeah.

RADIO:
In the end, waves
purchase a tale in theory-Greek
or property-Latin, saying none
of the above or nothing
of the flux of moving
figures to articulate
the landscape, to

reveal what's revealed.
A man who troubles
my parlor drama's nap
absconds

with his teacher to the University
of race distinctions. Incomparable
labor is his modern origin. The event market,
natural resource saving personal faith, emerges
well withdrawn.

OCCUPANT: No, no, that wasn't it at all. *[looking at INTRUDER's gown as if noticing for the first time]*. What the hell are you wearing?

INTRUDER: Football. Power.

OCCUPANT: No! Play the message back, dumbass. What's covering your body?

INTRUDER: Transmission. How do you say that? *[pointing at radio]*

OCCUPANT: That's my human head.

INTRUDER: Did you make it?

OCCUPANT: Almost. I was detained at the border.

INTRUDER: Are you there yet?

OCCUPANT: What did I say?

INTRUDER *[pulling a piece of folded paper from pocket, unfolding it and reading]*: "Every evening on the train from work, the voice on the intercom barked a ceaseless stream of numbers into the crowded air around her head…"

OCCUPANT: …because it loved her.

SECOND PLAYER: But she can leave that place where the wrong has been committed?

FIRST PLAYER: Protected by plexiglass and framed in distressed nature.

OCCUPANT: It loved her frozen mobility across the yellowing autumnal landscape that bulged and rippled in the buckling quarter-inch plex of the window. It loved the window…

THIRD PLAYER: Withstand the comings and goings of our cream-finished whatever.

FIRST PLAYER: Open the wall to show the facts.

SECOND PLAYER: It would be desirable the inspectors should come more often?

OCCUPANT: It loved the window, loved the message gouged into its surface by some unknown hand, which read, "I will teach ANYONE the secret all successful singers know."

FIRST PLAYER: Hello stranger…

OCCUPANT: It even loved the sharp teeth of the house key that had scratched the message.

SECOND PLAYER: Come home to the rigors of daily life.

THIRD PLAYER: Slip them on, then whisk them off. Sized to fit Bonaparte and the schoolhouse.

OCCUPANT: It was all for her. And her skin, each time she read this message against the flickering background of houses and shipping docks, each time she felt this unique and all-embracing love, would feel taut and shiny, as if the secret of song itself were germinating already in her blood.

FIRST PLAYER: Some of them cannot read and write at all, I suppose?

THIRD PLAYER: The message board. Or just random thoughts.

SECOND PLAYER: They get black and grimy?

THIRD PLAYER: It forms a protected area for the white spirit of vintage matchbooks and promotional postcards from tiki bars of the well-packaged hand.

FIRST PLAYER: Be careful, something's coming.

INTRUDER: [reading again from the sheet] "And so it was that one night she told herself the secret, humming the touch-tone melody of the phone number appended to the message which she knew, somehow, to exist for her eyes only and, finding it a perfectly charming air, went immediately home to pack her things. That very night she moved to a new city, one with many buses but no trains at all."

OCCUPANT: That's not what I wrote. That's not it at all.

INTRUDER: Then what are these *[pointing one by one at the words on the paper]* on...this?

OCCUPANT: I don't know. Subsistence. Export capital.

INTRUDER: The absence of evidence is not evidence of absence.

OCCUPANT: Are you quoting again?

INTRUDER: No, it is not correct. Sounds are making a guess with my mouth. Is this called singing?

OCCUPANT: No. That's what my human head is for. I have to leave it behind.

INTRUDER: And then you will sing?

OCCUPANT: Yes, through the holes in my head. You have not heard me at all.

OCCUPANT dials in a new station on the radio.

RADIO:
Hey, cutie. A man could
steal some money from
a country just like you.

SECOND PLAYER: Whenever one is furnished with a lamp cannot one read?

RADIO:
This economics takes
a look or two inside

the world's oldest, purest
teeth. The way

a hundred years hence
another planet comes
and lands atop a city.
Blunder, white as noise.

FIRST PLAYER: Elevated on its feet, our long-wearing ideal has hidden zippers.

THIRD PLAYER: Works double to serve a single person with preprinted daily erasers.

RADIO:
The right to die and be
the world is the bomb
in 50,000 planes. I mean
this as geometry, things

in a goddamn mess of
straightup wheels. Plots:
one is asleep at night, one's secret
Mussolini is afraid. And now

the oath to hold no
body naked, the brutality
of loneliness finding ways
to send unfiltered email home.

INTRUDER: When I do hear you, how will I know? Will I… "grab" it?

OCCUPANT: "Grasp" it? *[gets up and kneels over the toilet again, this time sticking head, arms and entire upper body into the bowl to search for something].*

SECOND PLAYER: Vanity offers the plantation house, in an antique white finish.

INTRUDER: Yes. Transmission received.

OCCUPANT [from inside the toilet]: You know, I don't think you get the difference. Grasp and grab, I mean. Or anyway, you won't *do* either when it matters. It'll be beautiful, though, and that'll be enough for you. And I'll have nothing to say. Ah, here we are.

OCCUPANT surfaces from the toilet with a pair of thigh-high boots in hand, then drops them on the floor in front of INTRUDER.

THIRD PLAYER: The item shown reflects our country's leading supplier. Hand-crafted of weather, metal, and solids.

FIRST PLAYER: Why should you distinguish them from others?

SECOND PLAYER [slapping a card down in the middle of the table] The six deep drawers of our aesthetic transform sleeping into sweeping.

FIRST PLAYER: Sorry, looks like you eat the loss on that one. Let me take it off your hands.

SECOND PLAYER hands the card over, noticeably irritated.

THIRD PLAYER: Be careful! A bill might come.

INTRUDER: All the calls are local. There are no charges. *[pointing at boots]* This proves it. Have you called it yet?

OCCUPANT: It's a reptile.

INTRUDER: I know that one. It laid eggs in my brain. I thought of far-off places and the people who teach people to make things. Are you there yet?

OCCUPANT: Not quite, that wasn't it. But something is *definitely* coming. *[turns around and kneels into toilet again]*

INTRUDER: I am not receiving it. It is not singing.

OCCUPANT [from inside the toilet]: Sshhhh! Come closer and listen!

INTRUDER: I am nervous. Water is on me from my body. It is beautiful. Nothing is covering my body. No transmission.

OCCUPANT: Damn it, do I have to do this for you? Come over here and give me a hand, I can't quite make it on my own.

INTRUDER [placing hand on back of OCCUPANT'S neck]: This one?

OCCUPANT: That'll have to do. If only I had more competent help…

FIRST PLAYER: When you speak of sub-inspectors, do you mean men at a less salary, and of an inferior stamp to the present inspectors?

INTRUDER: Yes, the human head.

INTRUDER'S arm suddenly and noticeably stiffens on OCCUPANT'S neck, forcing head into toilet. Gurgling sounds. OCCUPANT struggles up again.

SECOND PLAYER: Do you not think that the owner also suffers loss from an explosion?

INTRUDER: Yes, the margin.

THIRD PLAYER: Are they very anxious to see the law enforced?

INTRUDER [pushing OCCUPANT back down]: Yes. The call. The cost. Parties. Bills. Orders. *[OCCUPANT struggles back up].*

FIRST PLAYER: Some of the workers are keepers of doors?

INTRUDER [pushing OCCUPANT back down]: No, that is not it at all. You are not quoting. I.e., "football." *[OCCUPANT struggles back up].*

SECOND PLAYER: Why; is he a marked man for having complained?

INTRUDER [pushing OCCUPANT back down]: Yes. Reptile hand. *[OCCUPANT struggles weakly back to the surface].*

THIRD PLAYER: But he can leave the place where the wrong has been committed?

INTRUDER [pushing OCCUPANT back down]: Yes. At last.

Long silence, then the radio springs to life, as if tuning in a station on its own.

RADIO:
Wish you were
as terrible as this room,
but look up "brains" sometime:
a million dollars on a gaffe

or gaff hook. Sometimes
just monopolize, hundreds

of the white novels of defeat.
Today his handshake, tomorrow

the cuffs. An honor, really,
to have worn those special clothes.

INTRUDER peers down into toilet.

INTRUDER: Something is coming. That was quoting. The water has come to be very…beautiful? Yes. You made it. It is not making bubbles with your mouth. You are called…beautiful? Maybe. Maybe you are singing? No. That is not it.

RADIO: [announcer] Later that same day…

[actor] I can hear a familiar tune on unfamiliar lips, and read that familiarity in reverse, becoming intimately acquainted with the shapes and meanings of others' insides, their mouths and throats, lungs and stomachs, and how they sit inside those bodies. They all know something about a party to which I have not been invited. And at that party, all the lights drained from our frail and flickering streetlights create an overwhelming dazzle.

As the radio voice speaks, INTRUDER leaves through the still-open door. Tight focus on mirror, where PLAYERS sit in silence. INTRUDER emerges into mirror frame. Tighter focus eliminates frame: now we are in the room with the players and their new companion. INTRUDER climbs atop the card table, the long gown flowing well over the edge of the table.

INTRUDER: She spoke slowly and with great diffident gestures between each word and the next… *[drapes hem of skirt over FIRST PLAYER'S head]*…acting a dance in the very immobility of the language, as if every border were fluid and could be redrawn to suit her need for a dress that best showed her shapeless body to the friends who had long since left the theater, leaving with her only the command to eat as much of that functional space as her embrace of it might allow…

Cut to close-up shot of radio on bathroom floor, leg and one trailing hand of OCCUPANT on the floor beside it, rest of body still in toilet. Hand suddenly scrabbles around until it locates the "Play" button on the tape deck, presses it with an exaggerated gesture. Cut back to card table.

RADIO:
Later that same day,
same avarice around nothing
we can take from those
imperishable words: we hold
these cars in traffic, these
crafty enemies to our exquisite tunes

INTRUDER: …or as if each line could be rearticulated to cut across those routes *[draping hem over head of SECOND PLAYER]* that would best undress those same friends…

RADIO:
Webcast on the BBC, reflection
shines my bald head, just my
luck: the special relationship
gets me up at dawn.
The little stranger grunts:
"I hope you stop."

INTRUDER: …into the purity of their own fundamental enjoyment of what they did…

RADIO:
This nothingness, this image
To gladden hearts with
Gushing forth, and patients
In their strict confinement.

INTRUDER: …accumulating functional black-box buildings full of discontinued apparel with nowhere to go, and thus she did her duty by them *[drapes hem over THIRD PLAYER'S head]* for as long as every word could be treated as a block of equal size…

RADIO:
Marking out the limits,
Grouping things together:
The aim, the it. Again,
The word for what's disturbed.

INTRUDER: …and no friend would return to see her dancing there and believing in it.

Slow fade to black.

RADIO [through considerable static]:
Later that same day:
Are those wings? Do they
Bite? They fly
The world

Straight into you.

Later That Same Day...

Today the monochrome of the little television set shifted what it meant by saturation from black to red, and summer snow fell like milk on blood. Or petals fell on beach sand like the name of a departure that I gave to the patterns struggling to emerge there, "What I Know, Drowned by Flowers," in memory of my aunt and the method of her untimely death.

RADIO:

If I pitch my voice just right, time it to that "untimeliness" to which I seem to have been, for the moment, consigned, can you hear it, the almost cancelled compound of obliterating hydraulic machine noise booming in the background, and obliterated high and dry whispers breathing right into your ear, like the *rumbling noise, in the silence of the half-built freeway, of a bread delivery truck with a fly buzzing after it?*

> I connote multitudes, which town amounts
> to a shell of bodies. Twisting topos,
> intelligible form. Air's gone, lost in
> catalog's distracted secrets. Discrete pleasure,
>
> sucking collated cleansers. Eat!
> One lips such theme, is taken as
> palate all askew in
> stranger slang, prairie dentals. Back
>
> in waves, purchase. Articles abscond
> with tongue withdrawn to count teeth. Ways
> you die, the things one is
> not. No body nor room but lines'

avarice. Around command they stop
getting it. I want *their* world.

Well, anyhow, for all the mournful metaphysics keeping me at bay, or running down the hall to pronounce me culpably dead without once, as they say in another setting, "producing the body," it's obvious from what this "inquest" has let slip — an earlier episode's "flooded roads," so casually bringing recollection to an end, the present new beginning in an underwater archive, and the bit of tedium that went between, swamped in the shapeless wash of an absolute past built for display purposes alone, like an aquarium — that, drowned or not, we're all in a single cargo hold here. But the boy has never seen the inside of a television studio, or climbed the transmitter tower over on the next block, and so imagines "secret signals" as the chief export of a country far larger and brighter than the space to which I have been forced to retreat, down here in the basement.

Despite their tenuous grasp on probability — just now there was a fragment of a program, lasting a few seconds before it lapsed into the out-of-place and out-of-season winter landscape of pure transmission minus message, in which the action took place in the basement of a Florida duplex, as if such a thing were not a flat contradiction in terms — and despite, as well, the impossible community of post-mortal residues in which they try to implicate us, I meditate on these patterns of emergent image and *never cease to believe that they correspond to a reality independent of myself.* Of course, this seems to be the time for such belief, since these days I often awake surrounded by a new city, the park where I cut class to eat lunch the day before having turned overnight to a gleaming marble monument whose every surface has been scrubbed entirely free of association, while the grownups whistle by overhead, sucked around town through pneumatic tubes in translucent, pill- or coffin-shaped suspended animation capsules, resplendently unconscious in their snug mylar underwear, so that the kids all come to school with paste smeared on last year's pilled-up flannel clothes, hoping to win some friends or at least gain some purchase.

"But I know I was there only yesterday," one says, "if only by the stamp in the back of my library book."

By a supreme muscular effort, far in excess of her real strength, divesting me, as of a shell that serves no purpose, of the air in my own room which surrounds me, an assistant replaces it by an equal quantity of the mingled, heat-atomized sweat of all the other boys and girls whose names have escaped me only to drown in the general deluge and return as component elements in the all-over sense of subsuming identity, *indescribable and peculiar as the atmosphere of dreams, which my imagination has secreted in the name of* some country or other; *I feel myself undergoing a miraculous disincarnation, which is at once accompanied by that vague desire to vomit which one feels when one has developed a very sore throat.* The assistant, or assistance as such, Americana, advances slowly down the hall towards me, lugging the heavy water can for the dried-up ficus tree, while her other hand aims the remote control right through me at the tropical blizzard onscreen, and the breast pocket of her flannel work shirt bulges squarely with the new pack of cigarettes she has smuggled in to console me while I am grounded here.

Sometimes I hear a familiar tune on unfamiliar lips, and read that familiarity in reverse, becoming intimately acquainted with the shapes and meanings of others' insides, their mouths and throats, lungs and stomachs, and how they sit inside those bodies. They all know something about a party to which I have not been invited. And at that party, all the lights drained from our frail and flickering streetlights create an overwhelming dazzle.

Meanwhile, the sad hurdy-gurdy man of my evenings alone plays on the beat, but out of date. *"My old friend the policeman,"* he sings, unspooling a line of quotation I'm supposed to recognize into the nonchalant whistling from down the block, where before were only dry thuds of wooden blows against flesh, and with this citational lyric he dares the momentary lapse into civility with the most ambivalent of songs, whose every line descends to the very heart of the subterranean city where a constant mechanical blaze of activity sustains the placid demeanor of the block on which I live, and for which the storm drain, often cause for a bit of idle speculation, serves as waiting room.

RADIO:
This is not the blues. I will pick the basement lock, apparitional though I might be, to make him stop and realize that everyone has left, and that the voices he hears are the moisture-filtered automatism of a final tape collage assembled and left behind by a disreputable family friend in exchange for the family and the very neighborhood itself, all of whose members have followed his shoddy spectacle of a specter into the rumor of a new suburb in which the smell of raw sewage is not quite so pronounced, the dusting of distance purified into magic powder falls a bit thicker, far eyes light on farther thoughts, no glass, but on each branch a bird through which to gain a glimpse of the objective, more and more like inconsequential messages from an automated nature preserve both benevolent and thoughtlessly random. *These moments which he spends in my company, for which he has waited so impatiently all night and morning, for which he has quivered with excitement, to which he would have sacrificed everything else in the world, are by no means happy moments; and well does he know it, for they are the only moments in his life on which he concentrates a scrupulous, unflagging attention, and yet he cannot discover in them one atom of pleasure.*

Just now there's an odd lack of resonance in the chambers of the house through which the news of beatings used to carry, as if something were occupying more than its share of space in one of the hollows. Perhaps it's parents, or long-withheld siblings, or the neighborhood watch — for if memory is made of such things, why not experience? — coming away from the game of hide-and-seek I never agreed to join, and for which I certainly never volunteered as "it," and returning to the light to set their traps and link their hands in a human chain, shielding me from the hungry and probing, elongated snouts of the drowned corpses whose eyes follow me from every corner into which I have not yet gone, or into which I no longer dare to go, and whose rabid and subliminal chittering chides me for the ill-conceived, last-minute science project, the cruelly administered electric charges and hastily mixed reagents, the radioactive drift and spread of something moving like an allegory, that set them loose within the circle of a newly reduced perimeter whose patrolling carnivores were all buried in the back yard. Something, for sure, is on the verge, and the formal tones in which I am addressing no one in particular bespeak a threshold state of sorts.

I want the world for you. Sometimes I hear an unfamiliar tune on familiar lips, and imagine a nakedness for myself to fit the hollow of that mouth. Then I forget which of you I was talking about, regardless of the incredible specificity with which I can recall the entire expanse between the pearlescent lip gloss and the bit of scalloped elastic signaling panties just above the denim waistband, or between the translucence of a downy mustache and the telltale square bulge at the crotch telling of stashed cigarettes, and the more alluring expanse in which these terms have their chiasmus.

RADIO:
The dust in this room stands up by itself. Maybe we should go for a walk into thinner air.

In such an intimate space, everything bears the legible press of everything else: it's simply a matter of time. The ragged rip in the curtain over there helps me to remember an old comrade, Mr. Bird-in-Your-Hand, with the fresh stitches still cutting into the angry red flesh where the baton had struck him during an attack on City Hall, or at a concert, since his recounting of the one incident always overlapped the other in such a way that it become impossible in principle to distinguish the possibility of his heroic resistance from the documented fact of his stoned and boozy belligerence. There must be someone outside as well, to explain the soap bubbles drifting in through the window and disappearing before one can count them, leaving me asking the world for you. And by this image, in turn, I remember Americana, constantly adjusting the calendar to account for the way some days have of seeming to have passed without depositing anything more than a bit of weight behind one's eyes.

At that moment, I contracted my fear that what I said would be subtracted from the world, that words were pre-emptive much like news of yet another war on television, and that, *by voicing them, I should be excluding just those words — the dearest, the most desired — from the field of possibilities.* It is for this reason that I have accepted the reports which leave my dear Auntie Terrible for dead, and closed the volume in which it was possible to name the earliest recipient of — or fugitive from — my affections, by this means enlisting their services, these absences, as file clerks in the National Archive of Crank Pamphlet Literature, in whose yellowing pages and gradually demagnetizing digital facsimile storage devices they function as the continuous documentation of their own prolonged effacement. My habit of reverie is the largest private employer in town, since the port economy went south. A world of want for you.

RADIO:
He waits, hoping that we didn't mean it, and that we will return to send his hope scattering with a quick flick of the light switch. Around this corner, we should find a place to which his voice will not carry, and from which we shall no longer have to overhear as he finds occasion through his complicit hesitations *to have others play to him that music the voiceless rendering of which does not suffice him,* letting the nametags drop with a percussive rhythmic click into the desk drawer, to be retrieved casually by the surveillance robots as they scour the house in a frozen or submerged interval, setting the stage for the next moment with nothing to disturb the succession...

Like the other day I saw this guy I thought I might have known before, lifting up his house and building new rooms between its uprooted foundation and the ground to accommodate a roommate who would remain, for some time at least, just a few degrees off my line of sight. He had an odor called "One of These Guys I'm Gonna Call Your Name" that drifted thick around him, making it obvious that no one had taught him how to control its application by restricting it to a few well-chosen pulse points. There was a troupe of diminutive, itinerant artists whose work took shape entirely among the castoff plastics and bits of packing material that seemed to fall in a veritable summer shower from his always turned-out pockets. *A man may be illiterate, and make stupid puns, and yet have a special gift which no amount of general culture can replace* — in this case, the kind of rubbery and non-specific physique that left him on most days nearly as inside-out as his neglected pockets. But he is a fugitive now, and wears a disguise, drifting around memories like the corners ideology hails in place of lines, and this is not his story.

For the moment, this will be the story of an august personage, shrouded in the voluminous folds of a cape fluttering as a standard somewhere among the ambivalent sexual conventions of superheroes and vampires, who appeared among us one day wearing a nametag inscribed with the words "My Point Exactly" in a flowing calligraphic hand — words we took, in the absence of any language to sway our prejudices one way or the other, the stranger never speaking a word, to be the name of whatever body it was that resided deep within that satin shadow, a personage marked above all else by a loyalty to the concept of friendship so absolute that one might count upon that chiaroscuro figure beyond all concept of limit, so that, even when engaged in the murder of those very friends, dropping voracious nanomechanical demolition bugs into one's ear during an intimate exchange, swiftly jabbing new strains of bioengineered virus into the back of another's leg with a needle-tipped umbrella, or simply bludgeoning a third to death with a 4x4 pressure-treated post, the fatal act itself would always be seen, were there witnesses, which as a matter of principle there never were, to emerge from exactly that gestural matrix of voluminous flourishes and calligraphic graces which formed the lexicon of that exclusive little club, in a terminal act of devotion to their secretive and close-knit conclave so absolute that nothing else in the world could or would compare.

A rulebook had been memorized down to punctuation, allowing for the greatest possible accuracy in a situation where each embellishment of its text went just that slightest bit too far, and this was My Point Exactly. This gave rise to a condition of stiffness unaccompanied by swelling, as if the world were to be stuffed into the all-purpose suitcase of an indefinite article, and this was My Point Exactly. The contents of every such experience turned out, on closer inspection at one of the various borders it was always having to cross on business trips, to be a collection of severed heads preserved with almost curatorial finesse, still chattering amiably among themselves in a post-decapitation reflex that had gone on far too long for decency, and that was by now verging onto the grounds of art or public policy, and if this was not quite My Point Exactly, it always seemed to occupy a few cubic feet of space in the opposite corner of whatever room it was into which that baroque figure unfolded itself.

There would always be a TV set, in those heady days just before cable, tuned to a fractional frequency between two of the integer stations the rest of us received. It wasn't so much that our cloaked and silent visitor — or perhaps it was we who were the guests, since all that drapery had a way of obscuring the very basics of sociable geometry — put on those shows, in which power revealed itself with especial clarity among menageries of oddly asymmetrical animals found in still-smoking craters in the hot zones out past the Mulberry gypsum stacks, simply for our benefit, whether to instruct or amuse, but that, being rather more preoccupied with the flicker and whisper of that classified signal, as if it were addressed directly to the presumptive face behind that light-absorbing mask, than with the conversation we were able to muster in response, the satin-finished shadow simply couldn't be bothered to turn it off when we were around.

TELEVISION:

    Contracted at seams that swell
    armatures to frames, arms embrace re-entry's fire.
    To arc cold lumps from ballast, to tabulate
    so under brackish tongues, licking

    signage. While you're out, its aggression might
    imply just atoms. A stake,
    and the heart fled the matter.
    If fact's ass-backward, body'll drag,

    an issuer of interminable elimination.
    States border ends. Congested tissue's
    ample, and just meets a stake in
    royalties, singing at suggestion while it might

yet turn a tooth's weight to worth.
Bolt into the culpable works—away with you.

Grandma Violet heard in this the threatening implication that, in some grand scheme of things or other, it hardly mattered whether I lived a burlesque or was drowned in a shark cage on the legitimate stage. The difference was, in the eyes, somewhere back in all that hooded darkness, of My Point Exactly, entirely literary, which is to say it set up a pup tent in the public square or, since such a civic and civil architecture was unknown to our particular corner of the New South, in the remote sector of long-term parking at the mall in which a weekend drag-race would erupt for a few hours every Saturday evening before the cops shut it down.

"Whatever floats your boat," would come the inevitable dismissal and acquittal from one of the bagged heads, doubling for the total lack of speech within all that richness of superfluous clothing, and arriving early in order to depart ahead of my arrival at the scene of what I desperately needed to be a capital crime all my own. Talk about embellishment rewiring the appliances of tradition! At which exclamation in an interior monologue projected forward into a future of public comment on my current situation of unmediated experience, I noticed for the first time the copper screw threads spiraling around the base of each of those severed necks, and the puckering sockets smacking hungrily in the dark along the curtained walls.

So there were footlights, or headlights, and my spectator's pleasure was quickly consumed in utility and blind curves above the speed limit. And with my eyes fastened on that inconceivable image, I strove from morning to night to overcome the barriers which my family were putting in my way. Which was, of course, to emphasize the "work" in this "opera," bracketing the question of improvisation to concentrate on heavy lifting, regulated by exhaustive time-and-motion studies, stroboscopic film strips catechizing the body into a correctness of posture and a rote, mechanical exhaustion only in whose wake could the proper sort of prurient tingling be felt. There were little boxes somewhere near the edge of the scene, which you had to duck your head and doff your hat to enter, and which seemed to me the most magical places in all of a vast cosmos, their strait, dark and rancid confines the surest arguments the scenic carpenter's craft could mount for the reality of the heliocentric and hygienic vastness one had only, once inside the stall, to close one's eyes in order to imagine as the force arraying all one's awkward and gravity-defeated motions in an orbit only mildly eccentric and always sneaking in just under deadline. It was as if Americana stood watching over my shoulder as I wrote letters to a long list of political prisoners, reaching down every few words to strike through something she would characterize as "not a real word at all," if not simply "deleted for reasons of security." Then she would be off again, drawing a bath in the other room the thick billows of steam from which would draw, in turn, a rolling chorus of the bagged and socketed heads, of which one usually preferred to catch sight, if one caught sight at all, in the smallest corner of one's vision, occupying the slightest edge of discrepancy between, say, light as noun, light as verb, and light as pure elemental, adjectival quality-without-quantity.

Thanks to an arrangement that is, as it were, symbolical of all spectatorship, everyone feels himself to be the center of the theater, excepting he whose view is blocked by the slow inflation of a sacrificial skull directly before his own. What mattered most of all, though, was that someone should be on hand to congratulate me on making the necessary and reciprocal sacrifice with my purchase of the discount ticket marked "obstructed." But each peep booth, being absolutely interchangeable in reality, and staffed in fact with its own obtrusive, neatly severed reminder of the executions that were even then clearing one's view of a landscape free of any clutter but the clumps of scrub palmetto from which decomposing bodies were always being pulled, the series of such units of museum perception nonetheless occurred as a progression in value so that, wherever one started or ended up, it was inevitably the very next that held that lucky bastard who had the really great seat for the evening, as if one were always being taunted by one's superior döppelganger, who got to eat a last meal and share a bit of casual conversation with each of the condemned in turn. From this arose the habit of thinking of sounds as shaped and textured entities much like the blocky chunks of public art, so that one's failure to overhear might simply be made akin to one's failure to notice what would, in fact, be maintained in perpetuity for one's eventual disinterested gaze, a quasi-pyramidal pile of black marble, seamed like a cyborg heart, out on the plaza in front of some bank or other, dutifully keeping the beat. In other words, if my eyes have seen the final station of this train of speculation, it happened while my head was somewhere else. Some turn to writing books as a retrospective guarantee for the clarity of that perceptual "must-have-been." I call that acting, don't you?

By this same logic, we thought of My Point Exactly as a set of eyes inhabiting a dead, and in fact departed body. In the face of such a lack of response, such a lack of face — for it is, for me at least, the angle of the corners of the mouth rather than the ring of colored muscle in the eye, that makes the claim of faciality upon speech — I invented words, often faster than Americana could disqualify them or insert her vicious editorial [sic]. But the fact remained that here was a personage, unclear in all particulars, slipping through all the nets of description one could use to make however conspiratorial and bleak a sense of the world, but who was, without trying or even desiring, nonetheless, if not in charge, at least charged, so that the air around those light-absorbing garments fairly crackled with energy, a promise of the magic and power that lay waiting to take us up and make us whole once the plant at Crystal River got up to full capacity and our radioactive blood gave us the superstrength whose specific lack we'd more and more begun to feel. I would come one day, the ionized air whispered, into full possession of a potential named and held just out of reach in the bottle of heavy water left to me by my poor dead Auntie Terrible, bearing the legend, on a curling yellow label in a no-nonsense script absent any mitigating ornament, "Let's Shake On It" — and this promise of a value held in prospect was My Point Exactly.

Of course, the ventriloquist heads left muffled in the sack in the corner were chattering happily of the stock market and the beauty of its soft, recumbent curves, while those plugged in and thus more elevated tossed out maxims on aesthetics to float down around our ears, a subtropical snowfall more exaggerated than those that blanket their own proper clime, more total and abstract in its leveled features, its effaced contours, its softened definitions, so that we took the whole at face value and went shuffling through the papers stashed beneath the dilapidated couch, looking for the registration forms for the correspondence course on courtroom sketching. We found instead the deed to a property wholly submerged in the failed attempt to build a shipping lane across the state — a deed belonging to someone else entirely, but abandoned as worthless and brought to us, fluttering in through the front door, in the wake of My Point Exactly — and in this imaginary status of our neighbors to the south as islanders, honorary Caribbeans, a status that emerged without our having to answer a single quiz question on geography, the triangle trade, the blockade of Cuba, or the nuanced questions of *département* versus sovereign state, I came at once to understand the proper text of lyricism. There emerged with an even delivery, on a sharp note, and as though they were no more than the completion (but scored for a different voice) of a phrase that my father had begun, the words: "A cab shared is a penny saved to make the portion of the citizens of a metropolis without a single regular bus line, of which you will not hesitate, of course, to call a meeting, more especially as the members are all known to you personally and can easily make themselves available."

I felt that it was these words, which I was sure bore some intimate relation to My Point Exactly, without in any way "belonging" as a proper voice, for that was strictly out of the question, that would reveal to me the incandescent vision where now I saw only the dark and pen-scratched walls of a grimy stall, peering into my own narrow space from the hard, cold seat at its center.

"If you look you are not seeing, if you see you have not looked," sang a barbershop quartet of severed heads, the current to appliances around the house switching on and off in time with their song. "The body's full of juices cooking down to jelly, and a jelly's just a cube with too much heat, like tinted Lucite waiting to become a living room *objet*," one of them broke chorus to announce in the earnest baritone of the voice-over.

All that I grasped was that to repeat what everyone else was thinking was, in politics, the mark not of an inferior but of a superior mind. Certainly, the one who would come rushing into the room at that moment more decorated than ever with highway signage and honorific brand name tags would be, without fail, My Point Exactly.

"Oh, the stench!" whined a head, launching itself from its wall socket toward the window in the hope of breaking a pane and letting in some hot, foul wind from the landfill or the brewery venting its yeasty gases, but falling short, cracked and bleeding as if newly dead there on the terrazzo floor. Someone was timing all of this with implacable atomic accuracy.

Free Trade Ethnography: The Talking Head Addresses the Commission of Inquiry

…contracted into separate short valleys,
the feet above the head and under
contract, binding hand and foot with hands
on deck restraining movement in the grain

of wooden voice over current events. Those planks
disjoint a platform for the public to examine hand
and foot as dated measure of the merchandise.
The oarsmen down between the rocks indifferently

    crack apart or eddy down,
    indifferent. The boat bobs,
    a nod to sacrifice.

        And away we go.
        That swell along the
        concrete culvert drains
        the flow of current
        for the main event
        itself: public works
        ram whole hemispheres
        right down the town's throat,
        gutting it. Movement
        rots the body out
        with its currency.
        Everybody swells
        with value, pinned down.
        In your gut, the maxim:
        Nobody moves, no-
        body gets hurt. The
        motel room during
        demolition lists
        as "equivalent
        accommodation."

To quote from the report: "They have a catechism there. It speaks
the import of divisions of and in the territory. 'What is a man?' they ask.

'A man is shrunken, wrinkled, and dry. Thus he is preserved for transport. His ecstasy, over borders. With him are the ghosts chosen for another passage. And the representative spirit, plump to bursting with the juice of function. He shows you his handful of medals: your serviceability, his service.'" 'What then is a woman?' they ask.

'She exerts great influence and seems anxious that the streams of water meander on across alluvial plains. Or her influences wander. Or she builds a lodge by piecework, fixing fluid wages into all return. Uncompensated movement in her circle models the new orbit we impose. We are busy drafting the decree. Get back to us.' 'And what is this lodge?'

'The lodge is always abandoned, very often burned. This is brand identity, by which one fixes residence. Doubtless no pleasant place, it sticks in the throat.'"

> Our correspondent notes: "One clears the throat here, as one clears a field, or a check. The song:
>
>> *'This frames arms, this river,*
>> *as it arms the frame. This we find*
>> *on examination: such a portage*
>> *would be impracticable for us,*
>> *and we run faster and farther*
>> *with every passing hour to describe*
>> *the labor of such navigation past*
>> *the times we pass. Wave*
>>
>> *where the plunge is flow of stream and wave*
>>
>> *where waters crag and peak and pinnacle*
>> *tower wall and gorge. Then wave*

> *goodbye to clouds arranged in strata*
>
> *cross steep rocks*
>
> *gathered once*
>
> *into re-entry's fire.'*

So it's cool. Look, they got too difficult.
I induced a sharper arc to colder nights.
Look at it, will you? But one small matter,
on this memorable or misremembered day:

> What seems too vast, complex, too grand
> for the pinkish layers piled up tissue-like
> along the verbal canyon's walls,
> crosses the horizon and burrows into earth
> as ballast. It's a paper ribbon, miles long,
> a chain of bound departures down which flows
> a line of camps. A writing on the plain: forms
> only seen from windows in the air.
> Tabulate their numbers, while
> you estimate their shape. Tablature
> takes root, a call to music. Clear
> the grounding in your throat, and sing,
> uprooted, into the lack of echo there."

So our field op sold us down the river,
until a lateral canyon's red wall stretched us wide.
We walked the gorges flat. The river spread, a shallow
flow of backwash over our brackish tongues.

To some extent the latter are transformed
into labor, if only through the imposition
of a lip. Or two. Divide that number into
direct production of the social wage.
Count it backward for a while. The remainder,
or, less exact, what's left, is the object-form
of that "minority reality" to which we have attached
cardinal importance. As in: we count on its return
with spring. As it drives our majorities into economy,
and we drive it, first to distraction, then destruction.

        As it ceases to
        exist. As it is.

            As is.

Apostrophe S

Walking After Mid-Century

Somehow I had ended up outside in all the commotion, and was facing a different sort of hemmed-in space, one unleashed dog after another coming to the edge of its lawn to growl and dare my eyes in its direction as I tried to sprint nonchalantly down the street toward a door I'd left behind. Of course, this was a period in which state policy was out in front, policing new ground for markets yet to emerge. Someone said a magic word, shot a magic bullet, and the paved surface turned to rubber. *I myself am quite free from any suspicion of partiality in this respect since I am opposed to all innovations in terminology.* All I wanted was a bit of comfort, though had it come in a package named "infomercial," "docu-drama," or "focus group," I would have curled up inside its hot, stinky guts all the same, as if it were a large mammal, found fortuitously slaughtered in the middle of a vast tundra, as which landscape I often imagined the stretch of Fowler Avenue out by the Tampa Bypass Canal, its broad inclines of brushed concrete and reclaimed land a bit too flat even for a Florida landscape, and needing only the intimation of a chill wind from some northern distance to set a whole chain of displacements in motion. *My mother repressed a shudder of apprehension, for, being more rapid in perception than my father, she grew ashamed on our account over things which only began to vex him a moment later,* which moment, in the plastic distortions of the timeline along which I fled toward my room and away from home down a street whose moon accosted each of its dogs in turn in the voice of benevolent pedagogy, might well have lasted forever.

To glance up in that moment would have been to draw an irreversible analogy, as if one were to use the wrong marker on the exemplary dry-erase board, between the moon and the mask of My Point Exactly, linking the way each composed its flat surveillance from blank holes in equally blank planes, craters opening onto recessed surfaces that repeated the higher elevations' denial of light, whether blank reflection or matte black, as one witnessed the eye becoming the absent face's outward display of its own unavailability, and the unavailability of the open eye itself, so that, never being entirely committed to looking at one, it might always manage to look at one askance. Warning one against the practice of apostrophizing simply by allowing the prudish disapproval of others' voices to filter through its own silence, it became Apostrophe incarnate, behind its own back and in its own face, as it were.

Lost a block or two from home in a neighborhood suddenly proposing familiarity as the substance of a thinly veiled threat, one *believes the charitable tongues which, as you may suppose, continue to wag*, standing in for the tails on the much-less-charitable guard dogs which, just that moment, go still.

"You can do anything with men when they're in love with you, they're such idiots," came a voice through what must have been a window, somewhere in the darkness of a block whose streetlights had been shot out for idle sport, leaving such windows open on a prospect of nothing but blindness, hungry pit bulls and damp heat, to disgorge such voices, whose tone and timbre marked them clearly as members of the grim collection of detachments carted around in the travel bag of My Point Exactly — head voices, then, singing out of their natural register to make a plaint or challenge heard above the rumble of the mosquito truck and its endless circling, the grumble of the dogs and their stock-still angry quivering, as if this lamentation were the moon itself and thus the equal of any endlessly-deferred announcement from the stubbornly silent velvet depths of the diplomat's mask. It was then I realized that I was not abroad from my room and soon to return, but had arrived rather as a *supplementary person,* secreted by my own convoluted subjective relation to the contours of that lost living room scene, and that, were I now, by some unscheduled emergence of daylight, to find my way "back," I would confront myself at the threshold in a quite possibly self-annihilating embrace. So I passed the door I had anticipated until that moment and went around the corner to the beauty college, knowing that nothing works so well as a new and haphazard discount haircut to distinguish oneself from the new sibling so paradoxically younger and earlier than

oneself, to whom one is about to arrive as if oneself were the latecomer, recognizing in the look of him or her who stands just inside the doorway one's own foolish youth of just an hour ago.

Returning to the house well past midnight with hair tickling and scratching at my neck under my sweat-damp collar, I passed the front door once again, heading first toward the narrow strip of grass at the side, where I gnawed at the base of the trunk of the largest orange tree in the neighborhood, the only emblem of any will on our part to enter into that curiously murderous and territorial individuation that often masqueraded in those parts as "community spirit," chewing it down to a thin point as if I were a cartoon beaver and then toppling the tree itself, using my dull lockblade pocketknife to carve into its smooth bark, with its fine patina of green algae, the legend, "I have not eaten the boy, but I must eat, for I am a bad, bad dog."

Flipping the blade closed and brushing the last green dust from my palms, I tried my best to mime a casual approach as I circled the house to the back door, planning on entering as if no introductions were necessary beyond the introduction of my body into a space in which it seemed I had lived all my life without in the least preparing within it a place for myself, *enacting to myself the scene of this introduction with the same precision in each of its imaginary details that people show when they consider how they would spend, supposing they were to win it, a lottery prize the amount of which they have arbitrarily determined. The laborious process of causation which sooner or later will bring about every possible effect, including, consequently, those which one had believed to be least possible, naturally slow at times, is rendered slower still by our desire (which in seeking to accelerate only obstructs it), by our very existence, and comes to fruition only when we have ceased to desire, and sometimes ceased to live.* Thus it was that, looking through the sliding glass door which opened onto the back yard and divided the zone of interesting gloom in which the family sat, saving on the electric bill, from the zone of merely blank night out of which I approached, wasting time, I saw my new sibling, who would occur to me from that moment forward in the wearily mock-philosophical mode of the "always-already," leaning forward, right ear first, to listen to a story which appeared to issue from the hooded recesses of My Point Exactly, a story which, speaking from the very center of silence itself, must have graced this brother or sister — haircuts and hand-me-downs being what they were, it was from my vantage impossible to tell — with invaluable insight into the workings of state power and erotic intrigue, reinforcing my perception that here was one simultaneously more tender in years and more knowing by far than the poor measure of my own experience. There was a hint of moisture in the air, as if a president were drooling happily in his sleep, and an excited flush, as of blood. Feeling my nostrils flare a bit, I flung the door along its track and stepped boldly into the dim living room, throwing my arms open so as to welcome my new sibling and roommate (there being no bedrooms to spare), hoping to win, by this gesture, the position from which the magnanimity of the gesture itself must be understood to emanate, namely, that of he who *came first* and *opens his rooms* to one who enters as a stranger, but in so doing, I knocked a heavy, coverless paperback from the shelf beside the couch where the family was sitting, sending them all into a scramble to decipher what bearing the sentences on the page to which the volume fell open might have on the present topic of debate between the new arrival and My Point Exactly, once again and irremediably silent upon my entrance. Introductions and their aftermaths would have to wait.

 I understood that, while my entrance had made quite an effect, the effect was all there was, drifting free of the entering body that was its cause and masking even the fact of the entrance itself behind the bibliographical occasion to which it gave rise, or rather fall, converting the potential energy of the encounter to a cold lump of ballast, the battle having been fought, decided against me, and entered into the chronicle by the time I folded myself into a too-small child's rocking chair in a dark corner and prepared for the inevitable moment when one of the family would back into me and, thinking they had discovered some rare and valuable coincidence, offer to pay an inflated admission to the privileged affective states I carried in the air around my head as the sublimate of all the knowledge of the wide world I had managed to assemble for my own index, reading the travel section of the *Tampa Tribune,* its lavish far-right praise for the bucolic splendor and radical quiet of the pacified Honduran back country, while waiting for my no-frills student haircut.

"The trail just there," I almost whispered, hoping to see the words drift out into the room and rouse enough interest to turn a head or two a few degrees in my direction, without, however, coming across as too strident a claim on any personal attentions, *"was somewhat beset with thorns (which is, after all, only another way of saying that it was piquant).* I am speaking, of course, of the path through the plot of undeveloped woods through which I walked on my way home from the beauty college, the ripe stink of asafetida rising from where each footstep crushed a small patch of leaves, in the filtered half-light under the pine boughs where my complex emotions, emanating from sources far older and more authentic than I, and whose achievements in that respect I will only ever match in mimicry, might better waft around my head and mingle with the rank atmosphere unobserved by the gangs of young men who, having lost their driver's licenses in a string of DUIs, ride their little brothers' too-small BMX bikes out under the ozone-yellowed moon for generic cigarettes, homemade crystal meth, and unprovoked assault."

Of course, it would have been clear, had anyone heard, that I was talking to myself alone, and that this was *the moment in which a sane man who is talking to a lunatic has not yet perceived that he is a lunatic.* Realizing this in retrospect, the recovery of a catalog of gestures leading up to that moment assumes an exaggerated importance for me. Thus I work to repeat my own movements, to retrace my own steps so exhaustively as to void memory altogether (just now I am climbing an orange tree as the means to overcome its having been felled), shattering the links that bind one incident to another in the order of necessity, so that something totally uncalled-for and out of order might erupt, and that *this piece of gossip might enlighten you as to the incalculable proportions of absence and presence of mind, of recollection and forgetfulness, of which the human mind is composed.*

It was in this dance of rewound possibilities, a retrospective labor of sorts to open up the noise of crises not to resolution but to catastrophe, thus accurately understood as gossip, that I found my clearest image of My Point Exactly, being he or she whose refusal of address founded all possibility of these proliferating addresses thickening the air around the house like a multi-unit apartment building rising floor by floor above us, and whose lack was in fact address itself, muttering to himself or herself and creating a hole and an event horizon at the center of the late-night living room tableau, in which, if we failed to overhear what was said in that unreliable speech of absolute fidelity, it was not at all a matter of failing in our efforts to approach closer to the position of My Point Exactly, quite the opposite in fact, for My Point Exactly received speech in an entirely different set of coordinates and, more importantly, an entirely different time, from that in which he or she spoke, it being a point well taken only in being taken up and taken well away, leaving us, except of course the sibling who had managed to cross proximity into the extremities of distance at which a call could be received, in the curious position of those who lean too close and manage to hear nothing but the sighing of wind across a landscape unobstructed by topological features, a palmetto-dotted prairie whose occasional trees and corpses are all marked and marred by electric slashes of char, and across which a radical and stultifying synchronization keeps any sound at all from reaching one save the death of rhythm in the equal segments of grooved pavement thumping along without phase shift beneath the tires as the terrain presents its flat availability over and over in exactly the same terms as your own back yard, or the ceaseless ringing of a telephone somewhere just out of reach, and you know — though only if you come to it from the position of one, such as I was then, who has not yet learned to tell time or navigate arithmetic without a share of terror — that a slice of duration is missing somewhere, not a memory to be repossessed, but a lag to be reinserted in the sequence so as to bring you out of step with the articulations of what it is you want to hear, to touch, *taking time to make time,* and getting yourself and the scene you inhabit into position to receive the news from afar. Just as I hit upon the negation of gravity implied in this last pose, really a dance at great speed even if my body remained crammed into the tiny chair, a loud crash stopped all the clocks at 1:17 a.m. exactly as it started all the family from their philological reverie to turn toward the shattered window just over my right shoulder, their eyes tracking down and to the left from the jagged hole in the glass, across my body still proposing its leap to eyes that followed this inexorable parabolic arc from atmosphere through membrane to ground, where they finished, leaning down over shards of glass and a chunk of asphalt detached from the repaved stretch of road around the corner, into whose still-soft surface a message had been scratched: "Sorry I'm late. Stopped to eat the dogs for strength to dance. *Into the total that determines my ultimate satisfaction, I have introduced the memory of marvelous moonlit leaps of borrowed bikes which I assimilate to my own but which, after all, I did not ride.* If only you knew how closely related we are, how closely related to all this theater of beginning at the end."

Needless to say, the writing was small verging on invisible, and the family, minus My Point Exactly, who might have been still seated in the murky half-light of the opposite corner but was curiously no longer visible, even given the somewhat brighter light now available as the sodium vapor streetlight cast its sickly wavering rays in through the broken pane, leaned down close to the surface of that bit of pavement as if something were about to happen, and the near-total coincidence of this posture of theirs with my attitude of constant suspense and suspension, as if a journey were always about to begin which would prove decisive for my future prospects just as soon as a road was built at something other than right angles to the existing intersection on which our house sat, lifted this attitude from me in a bodily dispensation of lightness, so that I no longer insisted on the antigravity of my present posture, but clung tightly to the tiny armrests of my chair to keep from levitating. My father and step-father, triangulating glances at each other by way of an exclusive and studious focus on the chunk of road and its message, mumbled in unison, reciting a text they were that moment composing so as to have known it always in advance, "Nothing comes up from beneath the street except the irrevocable decision to remain there in civil burial, and that alone spills out to excess. Americana, why are there dogs left to eat in this neighborhood, when your report accounted for every body, compressed into the wet blacktop under the gentle and medicinal wheels of your democratic red delivery truck?"

"I heard someone clinging to the undercarriage," she protested. "Sure enough, when I parked the truck and looked into the mirror there were bite marks on my forehead, and a voice trailing off around the corner, whispering about a new number that would come and make trouble with all sorts of counting. With the currency itself in doubt, you can hardly expect me to be bothered with the nickels and dimes of a few stray dogs I've wounded but not quite killed." *The wholesale admiration which this performance excited gave an air of slight impoverishment to the one face we had to respond with, immutable and precarious like the garments of people who have none "spare,"* though the advent of a sibling had of course opened the domain of the second-hand, a new economy of sorts for our corner. But *the past did not yet exist,* and it was this itch at which I felt I might continue to scratch forever, never learning to read the movements of my life from the blank impassivity of the clock radio, which permitted no approach to duration and reduced time to unit quantities.

RADIO [noise for a signal again]:

    …such things to help remember
        manufactures of bread bring in money   supports of knowledge

point to point across the mid-state prairie, choose the one route there is
    to scale   maybe the mirror   simple as
      self-surveillance as you pay for dinner.
          And this clue will unravel in my domestic character

        such quiet conflict, for that purpose.
Precious ethnography. Charmed. Doomed.
But that's how it is: ornament devours
    a fastener tightened to furniture frames, picture frames and
    algorithms — ring modulation arrives, arrests a state of shimmer.
Start paying to hear utility   music to make people believe
    the destinies morning had decreed states somewhere

    astride the lips of giants, quivering
who disturbed the contrast
    won't be credible detail
and may not be much, but I'm limber —
        peculiarities of pretentious phrase   spirit capital
    followed pistol
    — I know the deal.

What's left when it's unwrapped?
Reading some entangled story:
Dollar, earlobe, breath — torn
with serial shadowy blossom of my hair
    his tiny body
    a boy killing lizards
      you order me

———

I recognized, sensed the reappearance of, the eternal common substance, the familiar moisture, the unheeding fluidity of the old days and years. And then recognition asserted itself as such and everything became strange at once as, looking out through the hole in the window as if toward the one prospect least likely to offer compensatory or phantasmagoric distortions to my eyes, every house on the block seemed to waver around the edges behind a charged atmosphere of garish color, bright primaries out of registration like the color halos in cheap videos. In the margin of glass around the hole I caught sight of the reflection of my new sibling, standing still for that long moment as if refusing to be lovable and demanding to be counted among the idiosyncrasies of the architecture.

"It's only me, Dolores" she said quietly behind my head, and somehow I understood all at once that this name was only one of several possible and that, given the oppressively synchronized rhythms beating the air into our ears, it would be possible to hear it always again from the same angle. But something in the scene was *tracing an invisible surface on another plane,* and as I turned from the reflection in the glass to the column of flesh behind me, forswearing the further elaborations of a dance I knew would never return to me, not even in my sleep, I saw him standing there — Mom was humming the song softly under her breath, thus permitting me the citation in a book she must have known even then I would one day have to write — laughing gently as he reached forward to touch my arm and reassure me, "It's only me, W.," a familiar foreshortening I couldn't help hearing as Double-You, leaving me wondering whether the initial at the end of this first sentence of direct address between us were meant as apposition or apostrophe.

"You look cross-eyed and half a second early, like you lost a little something out there, a baseball card or something else to do with counting."

Seeing that I gave a little start at this, "W" began, with a bodily calm that belied the frenetic speed with which the words arrived, to rattle off a list of numbers, percentages and averages, laying down for me a comfortably thick carpet of statistical noise that barred the way as I made a run for distant pleasures and anguishes, stuffing the aperture with the pleasant impression of a pillow dented to the precise shape of my head by long use, a little yellow, it's true, from the body oils rubbed into its fabric over the course of such a careless intimacy, but in that respect as well closer to the contours of my own animal nature than any swiftly-fading mystery of speeding bicyclists, dark woods, and televisions dying in the rain. Of ancient men and women garlanded with poisonous flowers living in abandoned alligator nests. Of moonlit sexual magic, hot nubs and ridges of swollen flesh pressed together through pinholes in the mildewed pages of discarded paperbacks. Of abandoned relatives, aunts and uncles I'd promised to circle back and deal with — and now this promise of no more interruptions, and I realized that I had been circling for some time, describing an orbit as close to perfect as such things got, given gravity, and that they were definitively and finally outside it, if they existed at all, and could no longer be so much as missed.

Beside the Point

In all this vigilance I had, of course, become ultimately complacent, lulled into a sense of permanent emergency that was perversely stabilizing and constant, as if I lived on the Tilt-a-Whirl down at the county fair where it parked, for the moment, off the southbound lanes of the interstate that ran through town, in the empty lot that had been until quite recently the drive-in theater whose outdoor pornography served a sort of pedagogical purpose for all the children like myself and my friend Vatic Bill — and perhaps now "W." as well — who had climbed to the asphalt-shingled roofs of the neighboring houses to watch, and as if, living on this careening and creaking, eccentric platform rushing through the great distances created by the evacuation of all those recent projections of wet, engorged and chafing flesh, my constant state of panic, the fear that I might vomit into air and circle back around just in time to catch it full on the lips and across the bridge of the nose, a displacement of the onscreen money shot onto my own bodily anxieties seeking any sort of resolving crisis, any event, however extreme, by which my interior might come to correspond to my gravity-distorted public face, so that I might emerge from a cocooned and awkward adolescence as the beautifully realized potential of one of the butterflies that had been said to inhabit my convulsing stomach on just such occasions — this fear, then, that I might actually have a solid center that would one day emerge, glistening and dull pink, into the light, like the disappointingly meager bit of bubble gum in the center of one of those two-hour lollipops in which certain kids invested the much-envied capital of their full-price lunches, selling them on the bus and going home giddy with both hunger and profit — this fear was the precise mechanism by which I kept my insides in and locked the outside out, and more often than not threw away the candy before bringing the blank time of my sucking to a critical head, failing thus to notice the imminent disasters that marked my route through each exhaustively and scientifically evaluated stretch of daily life, much like the road cones on the driver's ed course which the older kids seemed not so much to avoid as to entice, coming as close as possible to swerving around them before shifting their grip on the wheel just a bit, as if it were an involuntary reflex, at the last second, and rolling slowly over each in turn at five or ten miles per hour, savoring the gentle and forbidden contact with those pliant rubber forms, the soft sighs they let slip as the tires crushed them down around an escaping volume of air. So it was within this anxious lack of anxiety over the many disappearances to which I seemed to have been both witness and choreographer that a space opened up, the murky half-light of the opposite corner brightening just a bit as I moved aside from the hole in the grimy window and let a ray or two from the streetlight angle across the room into that recess, revealing that the motion of the shadowy rocking chair it held was no longer, if in fact it had ever been, the mark of My Point

Exactly at work among us, but only a series of approximations to the air currents of my stunned and silent breathing, paths along which I could be tracked back to my source, until I felt myself the focus of all eyes, a feeling I anticipated another few years would teach me to call Happy Hour. For, despite the terror implicit in this emergent tribunal, *I was now happy; my body had wished to secure exactly the amount of pity that it deserved, and, provided that someone knew that it had a pain in its right side, it could see no harm in my declaring that this pain was of no consequence and was not an obstacle to my happiness; for my body did not pride itself on its philosophy; that was outside its province.*

Perhaps it was some such chain of gut speculation that led my eyes to the row of heads still mounted, mugging theatrically in sockets all along the walls, and that led my thoughts back from the heads themselves to the nonchalant way in which Mom and Grandma Violet had been listening to their complaints with one ear and feeding them birdseed with one hand ever since I had found my way through the sliding glass door, and this path in turn led my own head down a descending spiral to the thick and dusty shag carpet, mirroring the screw-threaded interface between those obscene bits of decapitated social taxidermy and the very walls which my prior experience had taught me to regard as, if not entirely impermeable, then at the very least not shot through with contradiction and laid bare to a radical outside in which masses of headless bodies jogged placidly through the low-density subdivisions at night absent the intervention of My Point Exactly or, really, any point at all save the collector's mania maintained in a feedback loop between Mom and Grandma Violet as each denied any investment at all in the mounting stockpile of heads that came to decorate every available surface in our house, while the bodies themselves went on negotiating the rigorous twists and turns and cedar chip flowerbeds of the landscaping we had in all our innocence fortified around them, their steps guided by a cadre of Buddy Nation, Inc. Protective Robot Cross-Trainers, the discrepancy of this sudden vision serving to unsettle that of which I had said, only moments ago and with some certainty, "There, it's settled," so that when

I awoke it was to the flushed face of a man calling himself Doctor Duplex — a name I seemed to recall as if from a dream of political architectures pressing close in the thick and sticky air of some place in which I had been just before this waking — who was of the opinion that precisely everything was the matter with me, and who planned to hang out in my room for a while so as to treat, not me, but whatever bad lunch he had swallowed to produce the outrageous emetic symptom of his own broad diagnosis. I spent an indeterminate time in a delirious sweat: stuff was coming out of me, or was being spewed onto me, and a softly bumpy tongue lapped at it, pausing between strokes to mumble, "Yes, yes, you're some kind of butterfly or bug."

In the secret language of my fever, I mumbled more than a bit myself, repeating the single letter "W" over and over as if to retain some elemental part of the evening's events, but saw it inverted in my brand new compound eye to an "M," at which transformation *I realized that this imbecile was a great physician,* and that, basing my awakening experience of scientific evidence on an implicit alphabet, he had opened for me a proliferating crop of siblings to complement the one or two whose revelation only that evening had seemed so unprecedented, and which now, by contrast, appeared rooted in a primal and assured experience increasingly dispersed across the daisy wheel chatter of low speed printout which the doctor's voice mimed throughout my illness, as ascenders, descenders, serifs and counters ran through their repertoire of assembly and petitioned for a hearing. Americana would storm into the room from time to time, hoping to help me die but, in her haste, creating a draft which dragged scraps of newspaper in behind her, the lead paragraphs of stories in whose lifestyle sections were heavily underlined in bold strokes I took to be familiar, or else heavily crossed out in an approximation I found hard to take, the closeness of the leading making it difficult to say with any certainty what it was precisely my faceted vision was reporting back to me, news from the field of its own peculiar sort. *Now, a sheet of paper covered with writing is not a thing that the mind assimilates at once.* Nonetheless, I felt somehow justified in thinking that much of the brightness and rarity of the preceding hours had been deliberately placed in my path for some didactic purpose, and obscured behind layers of refraction and oily smears only to heighten my experience of discovering the already thoroughly annotated and indexed stretches of false fluidity in which, were I to drown, the Tourist Commission would have me converted to a divers' reef within the hour. In this thought, however, lay the death of my interest in the scene, and the death of the thought itself followed quickly enough, leaving only an involuntary shiver or two behind.

This consumption of consciousness by its own effects was perhaps what Vatic Bill had asked me to bear in mind as I embarked on a dim journey I seemed now to remember just having returned from — or should that read, "as I just then dimly remembered returning from a journey I seemed now to be embarking on?" — as he caught me by my arm at the crux of my indecision regarding proprieties of verbal tense and cartographic scale, whispering with a knowing leer, "Apostrophe has many friends, and one's address need not reach that mark to surround one with traveling companions."

To recall this conspiratorial promise in my present state was to confirm the alphabetic serialization of fraternity whose germ Dr. Duplex had implanted deep within my overheated, over-pressurized skull, plastic tubes and performative loyalties alike adding material and ideological ballast to my already strained inner ear, where fluency in the language implied by that script flowered out in a decorative calligraphy whose involutions and shadings brought to mind a stand of trees, oaks draped with Spanish moss and pines planted in geometric rows as if one were made witness to the grid along which wilderness itself was zoned for future expansions and improvements, the whole blanketed with a whispering fall of needles gone bright red in the bare minimum of light that filtered in past the edge of the road from the sodium vapor lamps, setting a half-lit scene that looked to me, *in the fineness of its grain, at once natural and supernatural, and in the strength of its skillfully woven tracery, a matchless work of art in the composition of which had been used the very grass of Paradise.* Smoking that grass produced the particular drawl that characterized speech in that neck of the woods, an affect I took to imitating even as I first recalled it to myself by its effect and further consumed the utility of what went on in my own head, suffering through the winding-down of my fever under the watchful eye of the good doctor. As if to confirm this act of retrieval, newspapers began to arrive unbidden on the warped pressboard table by my bedside, neatly folded and blown in no wake, but repeating the exact particulars of the marked texts which had been the artifacts of Americana's high-speed pressure differential, absent now the sense of an identifiable hand and given over to the larger scale of the archive.

Slowly, over the course of what seemed many days but might just as easily have been a matter of hours, my condition improved until I was able to begin the grueling work, still ongoing to this day, of reading through the prodigious stacks of yellowing newsprint that had accumulated during my hiatus, their sheer bulk militating against any hope of "getting through" or "paring down," and demanding instead that I approach them as architectures not to be reduced to my size, but whose heights of imperfectly-squared corners must be scaled, turning a few degrees with each step as the stack rises from the floor to some impossible place beyond the ceiling and yet contained within the human scale of my bedroom, as if they had combined the spiral staircase's decorative twist around the void of the body's imagined presence, with the Gothic habit of pointing upward and onward to that which summed the whole endeavor in an ironic perspective giving, in essence, an "A" for effort alongside an "E" for the ethical refusal of any sculptural perfection, the placement of the grade itself "off the register" in this respect being exactly what was necessary to teach us the habit of shifting the terms of engagement when quantity thus suddenly passed over into quality, as I was perhaps not the first to note that an "E" looks much like an "M" on its side to eyes still blurred with fever-sweat, and in that sticky blink acquired yet another atomic sibling with which to build acronyms like one-story cinderblock constructions arrayed at every corner of every intersection in all the neighborhoods my imagination of a grasp might happen to caress or strangle, rendering those landscapes familial if not familiar, so that the Emergency Water Management insignia on the side of the white tanker truck that came around at intervals to flush out the storm sewers when they choked on the bodies of the drowned and flooded the streets, announced to me not only my insertion in a world, but the hemming-in of that world by the cluster of sexy spectral siblings who translated its rush of sensation, as if it were a flood of stagnant and tannin-stained water, into an inside whose release valve they would always labor to provide by standing in the clear space just beyond and peering in against a great darkness.

FROM THE WIRES:
"D" for "domicile," "F" for "citizenship" —

> Is, as
> This, to
> Hang as
> Signs, while
> Numbers of

>> "Young Social-Democrats"
>> come upon the scene.

Everyone who I shall be shall be
"young" at the beginning. This, to observe
as "curious." Characteristic differences prevail
among them, like orthography or
out, it's *all one,* if not yet *all the same,* each
the aspect governing "mild agitation" spits it

can now imagine but the "federal-
bureaucratic" and the simultaneous
fight against it, strength there
is in authoring a letter dissolved
in contract. Congratulations,
we have ordered a mid-season run
of five episodes. Five stars: for
half an hour I shared my living room
with a clan of workers who "will not
understand" their syndication rights

    phrases propertied spontaneous against

and frivolous connection with
ritual murder among might

imply but also join them to themselves, subordinate a credit system, etc. Written: a volume of atoms. A stock meets another stock. They dance and fuck. Global rule is born, immaculate. It manufactures states, affects. How do you feel about the United States? *Are you glad to be in America?* (James Blood Ulmer). Global rule is measure, the spec sheet. Several billion fingers palpate the product into being yet again. How does it feel? Like a slow, dismal rain, atoms all falling in the same direction. A landscape picture indistinguishable from landscape. But there are several billion reasons to anticipate a swerve, a harmolodic curve ball. Democritus is glad. He pitches through that crowd. She's neither one of several sharp-eyed hustlers, nor one of several billion marks. Their fingers knuckling the ball hooked up to arms, limbs, branches, agencies, representatives in every corner of the world.

And the free trade of hostility, the mean inclining towards the state, crossing the median strip, the end in sight for our "Young Social-Democrats." The grievance, and its human face. A car to drive around downtown. If the face belongs to "our man on the inside," how do we see it? The reply trades articulation in the undercarriage for a body beset by joint pain. Remember that repetition is itself an injury, that *the peaceful operation of economic factors* drags by wrists, drags arms from sockets, drags along asphalt that meets flesh and impregnates it with grit more than skin deep, birthing value in the valorized locale. Drags back from capital all the way to capital, and farther back, to…

> No one really needs to say it. Monopolies flee
> majority. The weight of their fall drags
> majorities into line. Dip a toe into
> that stream. Tell us, how does it feel
> to be united, a solid state crushed together
> by the weight of die and presswork
> that crushed fingers from her arm?

Or, if fact's addition to its own suppression, then it alone is capable. It alone can wither away into herself. In other words: from whom it will emerge. Seventy years of that body'll drag ruined joints out of true. That's a fact, she says.

"Each wasted movement withholds music entirely," recited Vatic Bill, stamping my recovery with a motto and a mnemonic device as he sat patiently by my bedside, surveying and correcting the posture of my small frame wrapped around the deep body of the guitar he had brought to help me while away the hours, or days, or years learning the arpeggiated intro to "Stairway to Heaven," a song I loathed even then, but whose fit within my present experience, with its mounting successions of documents situated so as to conform to the axiom that "sometimes words have two meanings" seemed incontrovertible, even as it wrapped around the outside of that scene like a second skin, taken up in an almost-perceptible chorus by the gangs of men on children's bikes as the subvocalized talisman that helped to denature their longing for an unspecified something lying perhaps just beyond the parcel of undeveloped hardwood hammock at the far end of the street, past which even they would not venture at night, and in this function mirroring into a third dimension what I had to admit was its already-significant doubling of a hidden or unprovoked tangent neither within nor without my slow reawakening to the specifics of my own situation, in which a "lady who knows" could be apostrophized under the very name of Apostrophe, perhaps the single closing quote around a citation from another's dream that had occurred out of place to me in my delirium and warped my sense of the plane of my own time as if it were a sheet of 3/8" plywood left under pine trees in the rain to buckle and twist with water and stiffen with resin, wracked into service as an ascending curve up which I would have to pull myself *step by step, reason and memory already cast off like outer garments, and myself no more now than the sport of the basest reflexes.* All of which is to say that I imagined myself for a very long time balancing on the aching ball of a single foot, poised for an ungainly balletic leap into something as yet unfinished. There was, and is, however, a picture of it whose resolution is in inverse proportion to my own sense of irresolution at the time, the blue and white tie-dyed leotard inserting me into a physical drama about which I've always remained more than a bit ambivalent. Stroking my damp brow, Bill murmured encouragement and admonition to me, hoping to make me understand that trying on the costume was at that moment premature, since someone else was doubtless wearing a uniform in my place, the swirling waters of approval or otherwise streaking down her torso to bead harmlessly against the plastic harness, hanging one by one before dropping off the knobby end of the apparatus, a thousand tiny globes of serial reflection for the surrounding scene.

I marveled at the impotence of the mind, the reason and the heart, to effect the least conversion, to solve a single one of those difficulties which sub-

sequently life, without one's so much as knowing how it went about it, so easily unravels — that is, more apparatus exposed itself from the point of view of a hypothetical second camera. The scene literally took my breath away, leaving me gasping in an access of desire and terror all the more encompassing for its remaining, of necessity, unspecified, those sorts of magazines being only a dimly imagined allure behind the guarded convenience store counter. And then, from a near distance convoluted, pink and pearly, the light went on. Went on, as in continued, an assistant to an aide operating some piece of bureaucratic stage business having to do with the sound of passing tires on freshly patched and rain-slick asphalt just outside the window where the light as yet had failed to go, but sounds had gone on going past as our conversation did the same.

"He had," Bill continued as if nothing had happened, as if to continue were to send pink pearls of conventional wisdom rolling from his always freshly licked lips into a near distance where they caught the light and held it, holding it hostage, as in making it go on, *"a fair, silky beard, good features, a nasal voice, bad breath, and a glass eye."*

Things began happening quickly then, under the imagined gaze of this fondly remembered eye that could not be bothered to see what it surveyed, this intuition of a funky taste on the tongue and a ticklish patch of hair against the face, and so I found myself neutrally buoyant in the fluid spaces thus described, bumping softly at the underside of a shadowy outcrop that bobbed above my face as if it were a damp and algae-covered root projecting over a stream from some dimly guessed-at shore, and I a strange and hungry fish pursing my lips and darting my long tongue, as if a fish might be granted such a thing simply out of the desire to use it, feeding on the rich growth there. Something on me hung off me and swayed softly, and if it was my hair, then I was hanging my head back over the edge of the bed, a message on a bulletin board at the Park and Wash outdoor laundromat, clinging upside down by a single tack at what had been its bottom corner until gravity asserted itself as a memento of the absence of three others, busily adding themselves at just that moment to the quiet inventory of clothes stolen from the triple-load dryers, a disappearance thus advertised and memorialized in the handmade sign itself. I wondered aloud what had happened to all those clothes, both in the story I quoted for its illustrative effect and in the illustrated novel our bodies, patchy-haired, pimply, smelling expectably of stagnant water and incongruously of peanut oil, were busy writing upon each other, but my literary achievements phased in and out of coherence, following Bill's rhythm as he dipped his balls into my mouth and lifted them free, still connected by an iridescent arc of spit that refracted the humid geography and made its condensations real upon my lips. His cock tapped lightly along the bridge of my nose for a few minutes while we performed our approximation of the plumb bobs someone must have dropped to incise that very soft and porous geography with the modular elevations that gave our subdued athleticism its arena, until looking down to catch on my back-tilted face what he hoped would be the relaxation of intent into affirmation, a chemical reaction by which he planned, not only the transformation of my body by the elemental force of his, but the transubstantiation of his own in a reciprocal process for which my volatized face would act as catalyst, he caught instead the look of cross-eyed and excessive concentration with which I strained to look up at him through a field of vision thus divided neatly in two along its vertical and, pausing only to chuckle a bit, roughly grabbed my hands and placed them on his hips, testing my grip on him by gyrating his ass slowly above my chin, daring me to occupy the pose in which his choreography placed us by guiding his movements myself, and reciting as if it were the oldest and most questionable wisdom *"It is only people incapable of dissecting what at first sight appears indivisible in their perception who believe that one's position is an integral part of one's person."*

    I took the bait, or he took mine, since it was by now impossible to decide which way was up, and installed a puppet regime with him as chief marionette, his slow grind against me regulated by my standards of measure even as he governed my very breathing itself with his scrotum alternately flattening across my nostrils and hanging muskily just above, while my tongue sharpened itself into a point to jab into the flexing muscle of his perineum, and he slowly followed his own wet trail across my forehead, up under my hairline and back, fucking the flatness of my head as if there were some hole there, drawing a wet line from nose to crown that painlessly scored or incised my flesh to mark out the plan of a new dimension: you could have folded my face around that line like a spit-creased sheet of paper. In later years, I took to wearing the baggiest and least defined of second hand suit jackets, their hanging involutions making much the same point. For the moment, though, I grew bored and restless with the asymptotic approach and deliriously opened an entirely new line of questioning, interrogating his asshole with the tip of my tongue, a final declamatory gesture that was apparently too direct to be borne up in the complex of tensions that bound the sculptural sentence of his slim and coppery body to its draping grammar of innuendoes. He tensed and jumped free with a grunt that might have been disgust, though it coincided with another, involuntarily wrung from him with the sound of someone punched hard in the gut, and in fact he doubled over oddly as he came with great force and volume into my long hair, sticking everything together in a sodden lump as if to point again out the window at the fading sound of a passing car, saying, "There goes the operating manual for the bodies we used to have," in which "there goes" was both acknowledgment of something definitively past, and a demand that we hasten to catch up.

There was a sense of curtains drawing closed behind me as I rose and stumbled half-blind to the bathroom to wash my face and hair in a first intuition of a barrier between myself and Bill, a fabric drape whose contour the later experiences of my erotic life would teach me to trace in full and sensuous detail in the wake of almost all such moments when other bodies became a tactile confirmation of the necessity and volume of my own, which facts they registered in their displacement, ultimately of a piece with their disappearance behind this fall of velvet or asbestos, muslin or mylar, its lush specificity and capacity to linger over the scene making of it, in time, almost the very point of these ironically named "encounters," as if all those boys and girls, men and women were alighting on a tripod of legs telescoping down from a central ovoid body in some light-absorbing matte metal, searing the stubbled and secluded field of my nakedness as they touched down just long enough to collect samples so refined, so minute that their absence remained undetectable even to the one so robbed, or, on the contrary, scraping me raw and pink down to the youngest and freshest flesh shedding its tears of dermal moisture and mucus at once expressive and self-protective as if this were only the most banal of everyday events, then taking off beyond the atmosphere in a chrome streak of speed, leaving only that inscrutable glyph of burned wheat, or corn stalks, or dry grass, to narrate all there was to tell of life beyond the solar system, but beyond the darkness of night with which the residues of these encounters cloaked themselves the better to signal to me in their own deep and pulsing, radioactive glow, there descended a second screen or membrane, transparent in the same measure as it was impenetrable, which would separate me from the social body outside the window even as it disclosed it to me in its belated fullness and left me always to suspect that I had missed the boat, or the ride to the mall offered by the body I would more or less continue to have, but whose absence from my own field of experience I would take up as a circular lament to carry me, recursively, at last beyond adolescence and into something sad and paranoid, more like zoning than space. It was this sense of an inside that was one's own, but to which one lacked the access that the rest of the world blithely seemed to enjoy, to which Bill's recursive posture in orgasm had referred, so that our relation to the prospect of our own lives was lived curiously in retrospect, a condition surely misnamed as "straight," in that its shape for us — and, as I have come to realize since, for the spectacle of "the rest of the world" made so clear in the transparent overlay that day deeded to our perceptions — was a nostalgia accompanying every act, from the most mundane sorts of economic production to the most charged gestures of sexual release, a nostalgia whose coefficient of friction increased its drag in response to every lunge forward, until we found ourselves locating the image of our own sex and sexuality among the dead themselves, the muteness and inertia of their bodies being, we thought, confirmation of a story so complete as to admit of no exceptions, no qualifications, no asides to complicate the perfection of a narrative whose end was achieved without resistance at its beginning, and which thus had no need of getting underway, all of which goes some distance toward explaining our taste for secret meetings in the storm sewers, whose pipes were never entirely clear of the bodies of the drowned, even in time of drought, and which thus echoed for us with a silence that was citable as tradition and inaccessible as the twenty-year savings bonds with which weird and peripheral relatives made one's birthdays always an issue of the untimely. None of this, of course, changed the fact that above ground, fucking would always now carry something of interrogation with it, with the proviso that most cops wore plainclothes and remained indistinguishable from felons. There was never any question but that these questions would produce the confession whose syntax was always available as the simple inversion of their own, the kind of polar reversal of inflection one might accomplish visibly in a mirror, or in a tactile sense in the accidental encounter with a transparent membrane, the deliberate involutions of a fall or drape in muslin or mylar, or the complications of frame carpentry that managed to include the very sheets of plywood one had thought the eternal and irredeemable property of the vacant plot of pine forest, but all this agonized certainty notwithstanding, *I resembled what people wished for a time to avoid,* an interior horizon against which my recognition of this failure precisely of recognition would continue out of proportion and sequence with the passing events which sought to array it as a simple article against more properly hemispheric geometries.

Whether it was the word "array" itself that prompted me at that moment, still damp from the bathroom sink and having just resumed my melancholy watch at the window, to look more closely at the emergent suggestion of a pattern in the arrangement of lawn ornaments across the street, I will perhaps never know, but there, leaping out from among the riot of what I had taken to be a slowly accumulated scrim of scrap lumber pilfered from the ongoing subdivision construction site down the road, where raw material underwent a nearly alchemical transmutation into useless junk simply by virtue of being placed within a field where construction itself directed its productive energies solely to the building of its own future tense, into which it ceaselessly disappeared, was a certain Mr. Bird-in-Your-Hand, lapsing back into his old familiarity as Birdy as he broke the reflective surface of my rigorous avoidance of notice or mention in the aftermath of our shared history of failed attempts at telepathy, and whom I had thought to arrest at the exact point of our divergence by cutting off the water supply to the portable rotary sprinkler he moved about his lawn, making it impossible that he should ply his trade as a landscape con artist for any other than a wage, and ensuring that his own corner of the map would remain unworked the better to memorialize the look of things at the privileged terminus of my privileged relation with that aspect of his own privilege that he, with reciprocal rigor, declined to share, lashing out at just that moment with a length of motorcycle chain at a passing young man on a child's bike who rounded the corner just in time to be both stunned and entangled by this makeshift lariat, his mouth briefly open in a slack "O" of mild surprise framed by the even milder trace of a three-day mustache before he crumpled against the handlebars and wobbled off the road, dragged in by Birdy's sunburned hand toward the irregular stockade, which at that moment I saw again in a new light — perhaps the heat-haze had finally, just past midnight, begun to clear — as a subtly swaying, naked and inflamed mass of living bodies, men, women, boys and girls from all walks, rides and drives of life along the suburban circuit lashed hand to mouth to crotch to ass to face to fist, writhing and rubbing and humping in desultory if no less real ecstasy there as a decorative growth, some of whose branches he trellised against the thicker trunks to form a momentary clearing into which to graft his latest find, letting the sheer organic force of the mass of bodies hold the young rider in place as he came slowly to his senses, bent nearly double between two shadowed bodies as his mass of split ends hung forward over his eyes, giving his face an appearance oddly both demure and sorrowful, even as the same tresses carried out the most lascivious of mechanics, twining around the limbs that snaked around his own, binding the whole assemblage into place.

"You see," Birdy leaned back and shouted to no one in particular, though, living as I did at the odd number corresponding to his own even, I could not help but hear the better part of the address as meant for me, "the landscape does go on and on, even if we are reduced to inviting it home simply for our own amusement." I had to wonder, though, if one could still call "landscape" that which produced a separate vanishing point for each of its utterly atomized particulars by way of charging admission to the generality that would take it up into a horizon smoothed as if with a floor sander and elevated just a bare degree or two above what we took to be our own position as witnesses to the scene, an assumption itself made difficult by the very numbered mode of indirect address in which Birdy's claim to achievement in the aesthetic, rather than failure in the ethical and violence in the political realms, was made, so that one knew oneself in relation to one's neighbor's idiosyncrasies of pleasure and disgust by the segmentation that cut one out of their circuit only to scrape one's body like a thin layer of viscous fluid along their very plane. In such a situation, memory had ceased to be a surgical procedure, and could only remain as the evaporating residue of a water-based lubricant to which one's relation would be strictly indifferent, treating it as a means to a predetermined end. "Or a beginning," shouted Birdy in a final outburst already straining to be heard over the approach of that night's mosquito control truck, its mechanism incongruously strident in comparison with the fine mist of erasure with which it sprayed us all, "since *you will go on trying to discover what no longer interests you, because your old self, though it has shriveled to extreme decrepitude, still acts mechanically.*"

Bill and I, as rigorous in our avoidance of each other's eyes as we were in constantly checking the alignments of each other's face to hedge against the chance that we might be, in the blind spot opened by that very avoidance, accidentally and disastrously fixated on the same object, nonetheless took to heart as one Birdy's anguished cry of triumph, which is to say we placed it at the core of the fluid spaces and distances presumed and constructed by fluid mechanics in the sexual near-miss that, passing between us, had displaced our mutual center of gravity and warped the ellipse we had almost managed to form — his body curving abruptly forward and flattening his gut against my forehead as my tongue uncurled into him — until every moment of desire, every gasp of breath, every shiver of loose flesh at the corner of an eyelid or bunched and furled in the scrotum, every hard clench deep in the abdomen would have to traverse that evacuated space, into which we now realized — too late, thanks to our mutual refusal of any mutual perspective — had been inserted the totality of collective potential for the production of bodily appearances invested in a topiary social organism which the view from my window invited us to examine in full, at all moments, in all the deeply dissatisfying complications of its sweaty and self-involved surface. *With our love had vanished the desire to show that we no longer loved,* leaving us stranded singly always a few pages back of the advancing plot and wandering a void dense with discards, a waste or patch of scrub woods from which, as it turned out, I had only managed to emerge out of synch, signaling to our gazes as they obliquely angled past each other into fever-warped space just how deep inside the whole mess of slash pine, abandoned plywood and faded zoning notices we remained, and how little we had managed to see.

Survey Markers

The Parcel

This will be a long walk. They showed me through and now it ends in dreaming back to light. Let me tell you now there's nothing to hear. The noise of bulldozers and stump grinders covers an entrance. All our talk is of cover-ups and plots. *And so it is not wrong to speak of hearing a thing for the first time.* This is as sad as the work of collecting. Numbered parcels of scrub woods produce time for counting. We use the word development, voting on its measures as an abstract show of faith. It won't work.

It's *a sort of vast news item of which you get a hint here and there.* Light to produce your reflection comes from that source and shows you at your least essential, like a tame bird. Someone's burning.

Picture these words as bound parcels containing history. Before the men dragged him out from under his pine and doused him with gas, the neighbors had addressed their solidarity to him in the exact measure that it remained undelivered, or undeveloped. He wasn't such a sweet-natured guy after all, they said, recounting how he had bitten at the hands that circled around, receiving his light to warm their palms. The cop around the corner is missing a thumb and *doubtless, in such perfect coincidences as this, when reality folds back and overlays what we have long dreamed of, it completely hides it from us, merges with it, like two equal superimposed figures which appear to be one, whereas, to give our happiness its full meaning, we would rather preserve for all these separate points of our desire, at the very moment in which we succeed in touching them — and to be quite certain that it is indeed they — the distinction of being intangible.* This walk goes on so long because philosophy as the bird flies is joy in speculation. Here is a mirror in which nothing equals anything else. So there's nothing to hear. It recedes because it's present to receive you like a chair. I'm sitting on a busted TV set in the woods at night, picturing history.

TELEVISION *[hypothetical program]*:
[emcee]
...as the Man hatches friends! *[raucous studio applause]*

[dialogue in cop car, camera mounted in backseat as if for a ride-along, or as if under arrest]:

       Side of the bargain's accredited
          sentence   labor   spasm
        scaled *so long* to the mirrored case
habit's kind stand-in for the ally one considered
indispensable blemish   burst of grain along
           grasp   more general noise knots
             muscle   front & center in the stereo picture
  Wet years' achieved answer
            dry   distant winds

              drowned in radiance all visible distinction
    Dockside crane climbs capitalized hill in fog
    Scaled mirror so long becoming simple
      dust-free clean room   deep low-end reverb funk
          either long unpaved or finally rebuilt
         lubed   precision unemployment
Scenic money overflowing money, money

           keeps her forgotten in the distribution
perpetual scatter broken as your chore
        at every crosswalk   *make a moving*
        target learning to forget
  pronunciation   price of native innocence

> *of a cast-off gun*
> In far-off space   small homogeneous time
> forcing the pageant by
> which to make it pain
> Particular felicities there within the style
> *mean subjective pronoun daddy*
> *his tiny body*
> other nametags rushed sibilant past

So there's a person here I'd like to show you but the light is all wrong. When things are held in this reserve we call it underdevelopment. Come here I'm leaving. It works only as anachronism or inactive vacuum making space for a seat atop it. *It will be down below or nowhere at all.* We use the word apostrophe, as in making someone else open your mail and write your name and address on the flyleaves of library books. I don't get it so I know it's bad, and the plot of our talk details cover-ups. This is how — and the exact degree to which — the underdeveloped parcel is our freedom.

Parking Structure Groundbreaking Ceremony Today

Unburied lines that mark unexcavated
tops of walls. Local color softening
the marks of lines — of march, of flight, of
demolition and the last half-century's

highway projects *Scajaquada Expressway*
Buffalo New York Crosstown
Expressway Tampa Florida Major
Deegan Expressway New York New York
Cypress Freeway Oakland California — lines buried
still half, at least, alive. Buried *as* line,
at least, if standing ground still as burial in view:
beelines down the block now literally smothered,
tunneled unseen underground. *And the manifest ill fit*

...

And the ill-fitting manifest
of ingenious and puzzling contrivances,
destined, shipped, to whose overdrawn account?
Undermine each object, solid in soft daily shadow,
with prescriptive mechanism's hidden blockade of gleam
and glare off structural steel and new concrete
in plain sight, as every year another basement
falls to newer depths, someone's older cellar opens
up again the mislaid hole in jigsaw grids of
stones both old and new, crushed and cracked to fit.

Or the depleted water table sets
a sinkhole to consume the dining room.

Illustrate the substitute expense of place, in place, by means of place.

Ash garners full accord with all such late-developed exigencies:
the year they burned the hotels down San Francisco California
1999. That predatory rancher type, possessed of great reversions,
and the presence of a grille or two, whether chromium corralling
reflected and deflected downtown ambiance into slick liquidity event,

or, cow-catcher-style, cold metal grate of shoulder and hot
                              coal-burning fang,
plowing and chewing through railroaded, inconvenient land

— which echoes back reports of reputation, gulch and gully
of topography's involvement unfolded to a sounding board
or flat, low bed of fertile valley real estate on which to rest
some precepts, necessities of spending it to make it git along.

   In any case the compass of "pecuniary decency" withdraws
as much as may be substance from the class it studies "in the field,"
culture workers' weekend volunteer brigade recording work
songs, as the discount bricks of tapes build institutional

               memory of a pain in
               the ass the neck the
               back the shoulder the load
               bearing wall buckles and shifts
               ground that runs downhill as
               air oozes down the wall
               condensing space in unconditioned absence

of a breeze. Such closeness. Such
impeded circulation seems to be the fact,
that priesthood of cincture with its accent
on the earnings of the living, the fall

"by chance," one says, into the other hand's mechanical
                                                    rank,
the other's hand high up the wall, awaiting mortarwork
to level it. Shooting into air or raining down debris
— too soon to tell what adds up to adaptation
to a "new economy" of virtualities of space,

where "rental loss" stands in, not for secret
lunar room rotations in the SRO, but the *more*
a landlord might have made in public spectacles
of speculative fiction, were his hand not stayed.

In other words, exposure situates
crystal receptions for the business news.
Survival relocates from the fields and shops of process
to become itself the product, outcome of exceptional
chance procedures, favorable weather, *whether
or not* being what stays, in fact, the matter. More words
expose more situations growing tighter, more precise
within the half-hour confines of a market squeeze.
The punch line is the juice without a working outlet,
or outlet minus juice. Each day it gets a little
wetter, though, that condensation on the walls

        what comes of pressure.

Submersion comes in turn of it. We echo-locate lovers,
spouses, roommates, become aquatic animals, sounding
out, feeling out, the chilled-out dark in flooded coastal caves,
the casual connections X'ed out in classifieds,
thick description filling in the vacancy in lungs.

Not that fresher water would have saved you, that year
they killed the river *40,000 gallons phosphoric acid
solution Gardinier Phosphates (Cargill) Alafia River
Hillsborough County Florida 1988*. Or proved
that point again. Some places die like a refrain
*54 million gallons phosphogypsum process
water Mulberry Phosphates Alafia '97 two days'
drift downstream to enter Tampa Bay,* a "plume."

By ornament we learn the essence of a work.

Tide and rocks abrade us, wash us out to sea
—   salt-cured, in that wet lack of terminus, of *what*
slow-burning, terminal disease? — scrape our skins clean,

                infantile and hairless when we die.

The Plot

Come here I'm gone. I set out through this plot of woods to change my name and address cheaply, by something like a haircut. The first person here is not myself but a feverish little critic whose hair falls out with bloody roots from a ragged scalp that shows bone. People are mostly small and sick, disappointing as heroic figures. They make me sleepy as a battered head fully occupied with memories.

"We have to work at everything," says the little critic as if drowning. *I'm ignorant of what is to be done with it but firmly determined not to let it enter my mouth.* I see how it clots there, how he gurgles. It's an exact description of the person I can't introduce to you. Leaf mold and manure. Out of exhausted substance grows this mouth snarling to devour the flesh of my tongue. When he parts his lips the moon disappears. *However characteristic it may be, the sound that escapes from* that other person's *lips is fugitive and will not survive the little man of letters.* In his sleep he scratches lines into the bark of the oldest trees at the fabled center of a plot. The plot is marked for development by associations free and otherwise policed. That's a different matter.

"Making matter differ," he says, "makes it cease to matter." His mouth thus spins the whole plot on a pivot of moonlight reflected in the thick plastic glasses of *that other person*, who goes away from it. The sequel is a letdown.

The great thing about the derivative freedoms here is what they open to deliberation. Right now I'm choosing my own kinks. When they appear reflected in the dead glass of a junked TV there's no excuse. This is so much fun that the little scholar and I drown in our contemplation. This approximates the good, ever since I've "decided" to enjoy being held down and handled. The moon is very heavy. Everything being a different matter here, the trees ease down on top of me like slowly rolled logs or journal entries.

Given the heat of the climate, and the memory of fire, would it surprise you if I spoke of each step on this walk as something flash-frozen? Even the nearby ocean is pedantically shallow. Cast a cold enough eye and all mobility ends up confined to a sludgy bottom where discarded plastic dolls feed displaced dreams of overturn on motor oil, household ammonia, and phosphate runoff. This is my point exactly: a revolution that settles for art history corresponds to nothing. Slightly inland, in the waste woods, nothing corresponds at all but an informal and undercompensated flesh trade. Filtered moonlight just suffices for surveillance. Each skin becomes the perfect replica of the one *that other person's* ventriloquizing story taught you to desire. But without a wart, a running sore or infected boil to set off the successive generation of overdubs, nothing corresponds. Motion freezes from the top down to all but the darkest margin of bottom. There is no middle path. We shuttle between extremes. Wow and flutter mar the tape.

"You've changed," says the cultural critic, whose long promised withering away expresses nothing but what corresponds to the time clock. Having an idea won't suffice to own it. The words remain an accusation in his mouth.

"I love your lips and tongue," I say to him, "because they disappoint me more than any other lump of flesh you have to offer." We're facing the same direction, waiting for the same silhouette to be spotlighted by the moon. We don't correspond but collide, as the crowd here bangs us around.

The plot teems. It's unoccupied. You're always waking up to the object status of your body. Nearly as often you nap through the legislative protocols that govern its posturing. In the new translation, "standing congress" is "fucking upright." You're left with a real experience for the world to falsify, not a fake to realize in the treatment. People here grope each other's entrails to extract the undeveloped negative of the future. *A few years from now I will answer: "I never repeat things."* I know the family I'll return to. Who wants to bet we won't qualify for the benefits package attendant on such a fancy-dress occasion?

Of course, diplomacy would lead you to expect a horizon of intelligibility for these fallen leaves and mulching needles of diffuse impression. When you swallow poison you open your mouth and bark. Amateur philosophy won't console the survivors who forgive it. Pleasures remain to be renounced. I might shave my head with a discarded razor and burn the cuttings in a bonfire of delaminated tires and junk electronics that bursts out unannounced in a clearing. There would be women here who don't care to know me. An old man blinded by the glare of flames on his dark shades pours motor oil on their hair and scalps, extracting ticks.

"The things of the world have a different virtue here. Take this back with you and the world would be helpless," one of the women says into the smoky, humid air. Her words aim not at me but at my distraction. A second member of the camp gives my right ass cheek a sharp slap while a third lifts the wallet from my left back pocket to fling it on the fire. She tastes with evident pleasure the acrid fumes of cheap leather, state-issued ID, and cash. I tell her I'm hungry, and now anonymous and broke as well. The heat from the fire makes her salivate. She spits copiously into my half-opened mouth like a bird.

Though conducted in silence, this exercise was none the less a conversation and not a meditation, my solitude a mental social round in which it was not I myself but imaginary interlocutors who controlled my choices of words, and in which, as I formulated, instead of the thoughts that I believed to be true, those that came easily to my mind and involved no retrogression from the outside inwards, I experienced a sort of pleasure, entirely passive, which sitting still affords to anyone who is burdened with a sluggish digestion.

I've decided on a course of action. A benevolent American automatism. Guess which one it is. Come here I'm absorbing the surplus value of your concealed image for therapy.

"You're inside me as an arrhythmia," I coo to the spitting woman.

"Think again," she laughs, not in response but as an infinite judgment, dancing far away into the spaces closest to my skin.

Much later she writes, in correspondence across that distance, after all that has transpired between now and then, "If you'd ever come outside, you'd find that most of us are living under interdict at the borders articulating real states and capital flows, while you continue playing haplessly with dolls to one ambivalent side or other of barb-wired rivers, blockaded straits, and green lines."

In vain do I say: "I thought the other day that the clock was too slow, if anything." Perhaps this is what prompts me to a new resolve, writing by return post only to those I've never seen, or will never see again:

Dear Two Gray Sisters More or Less:

We are incapable, while we are in love, of acting as fit predecessors of the person whom we shall presently have become and who will be in love no longer. The low density of the city is an architectural argument against visible urban homelessness. Tents and lean-tos here are the undeveloped negative of that city. In the sheltering labyrinths of an underdeveloped plot of woods, I realize that this social knowledge is what I closed in on when I addressed you in the figure of an oscillation between disavowed elsewheres. This mobility is a site from which to phone in your translation.

There are people here to whom I can't introduce you. They hold their breaths full of acrid tire smoke and wait for you to join their camp of militant lovers. *We are not unhappy, except one day at a time.*

Our modernity is the way the bonfire has of throwing into sharp relief what's soon to be archaic.

That you can always count on meeting in this clearing people to whom you can't be introduced should help you get a grip on just how late the hour is. Think of it as an upholstered interior in which the treatment will play itself out. *"One simply can't tear oneself away from this house,"* is how the local enforcer or political officer wants me to put it to you. We hang out under boughs that drip their sap onto the fire. This will have to do for lighting our exposures.

The other day I managed to pull the officer aside and ask her name. Her response should be of interest in your present course of study: "I have to swallow a lot just shaking hands with anthropologists like you. *You have only to be in my camp five minutes before my fingers are itching to stroke your hump. That's how history comes to be written,* how the travelogue has to cross a greater distance than the traveler does. Here, let me introduce you to the Reaction. They're more your speed."

The gesture cloaked her in feathers, echoing an airborne and arbitrary path among the trunks and boughs that, in opening up for her, would remain over my head, so that the armament of imperial speculation with which I'd made my way to this plot, once commanding in the height of its error, now saw power molt away, leaving only a plucked, naked idiocy to shiver as the night breeze blew around the fire.

Later that night a doctor from County Health showed up to harangue the camp about a plan to bank panhandling earnings toward some sort of market-driven mutual aid society.

"Yes," answered the political officer, deadpan. "I believe you. Everything anyone says about this place is a matter of life and death. So kindly shut the fuck up."

The credo took root. It's now a nationalist movement. A length of salvaged dropcloth, stretched along the trees on the side of the woods facing the commuter highway, bears the charcoal legend: "KINDLY SHUT THE FUCK UP." *When we are in love, our love is too big a thing for us to be able altogether to contain it within ourselves.* But that's a dodge, like saying it's only the dime rock someone smoked that made her need a flag in the first place. They (we?) in fact need the banner not to name themselves — ourselves — but to name the others. There's a constant stream of traffic rushing past and taking things as signs along the way. That ascetic avoidance might be anything. It's not a sign. Thus the banner.

Perhaps I write to you in order to create delicious misunderstandings that will render me edible. I hope to settle your digestion of my own erring analysis. Many of the campers are clothed in the gnawed remains of just such a meal. At one time they even produced its refreshments, but that was back before the brewery started outsourcing beer. In the photos I've enclosed the effect is one of an unfortunate fatigue. But you must remember that this nation is so young it has not yet discovered its youth. It only appears wreathed in tatters and strips of the outmoded or attenuated. Passing by way of sartorial falsehood, you must come to imagine the truth of a new collective body still barely veiled within it. Then distance comes and spills into its folds.

Some design carried out in color which pursues across an inserted panel a preconceived existence of its own. The covers all stuck to the mattresses. Nowhere to sleep. *The deferred interview in which we would have to deal with a person to whom we could no longer dictate at will the words that we want to hear on her lips, but from whom we can expect to meet with new coldness, unforeseen hostilities!*

We sit on old TVs. We picture history. We build fires. I hear bulldozers revving their engines. The voice of everything familiar forecasts rubble.

Yours from the bright rumor of war,
T.

Closed Captioned

no nucleus is good
form along havoc you mattered
and/or minded *I did* and what
matter aim's to bend all

into shape quiet conflict product
of eaten center law of
extruded plastic instability manufactured
at global scale *my many selves*

various uniform as if buttons themselves
could sew connect connects and so
then meanwhile so sold solid
line descends to very heart

far eyes no glass but on
itself the arrow trained a row of shelves

Dear Surveillance Photo Aged by Speculation:

"I did not drag my father beyond this tree." *Because I believed that my sufferings were not destined to last, I was obliged, so to speak, incessantly to renew them.*

Whatever happens, happens in the intervals separating frames in the undeveloped negative. Memory remains a privileged access to subjective plenitude, but it's the plenitude of my own flickering discontinuity, a mobile translation phoned in on the hour.

A single rose or a Japanese iris in a long-necked vase of crystal into which it would be impossible to squeeze a second. And then another.

There is luxury even here — especially here — but no one to take the curatorial interest that might guarantee its retrospective clarity by defusing its explosive force. Everyone's busy writing letters to someone else. No one knew you were coming. Knowing bet the bank on it. I have kept on with the present epistle despite the band of women and a few men who wring their oil-soaked locks and squeeze their running sores onto the page. They dismiss my address to a surveying outside as "trouble with the help." All at once the great distances covered in the travelogue collapse into a sense of neighborhood.

You're lucky to be able to hold yourself back; I do envy people who can hide what's in their minds. Nonetheless there's a whole class of go-betweens who simply don't care. They show it to me with impeccable disinterest on the dead TV screens every evening. These are the arts to which the zoning plat itself attaches such paramount importance. *They do no more than discriminate between shades of the non-existent, sculpture the void, and are, strictly speaking, the Arts of Nonentity: to wit those, in a local enforcer, of knowing how to "bring people together," how to "group," to "draw out," to "keep in the background," to act as a "connecting link."* I wonder if they fear incursions of cops, out here beyond the reach of law in the bare wastes of political economy? About as much, I'd think, as anyone in this region fears a hard and lasting freeze. We bring to the occasion all the speculative terror reserved for a disaster so rare as to escape history into myth, yet so total as to depart by the other door into amnesia. Thus the reach of law extends. *I know something about it, because the hostess has a habit of pointing a pistol to your head.*

"Relax," she says to me, seeing what I've just written, "I shot your sorry ass twice today and you didn't even look up from the notebook.

We seem to need each other alive out of sheer boredom."

This feeling radiates towards the loved one, finds there a surface which arrests it, forcing it to return to its starting-point, and it is this repercussion of our own feeling which we call the other's feelings. When you have a feeling for the negative, though, this affective sleight-of-hand approaches class suicide through the alley entrance. *The time which we have at our disposal every day is elastic; the passions that we feel expand it, those that we inspire contract it; and habit fills up what remains.* Languishing in the enjoyment of your own feeling of guilt is one thing, but finding that feeling directed back at you — not only the guilt but also and emphatically its enjoyment — is something else entirely.

Her animals carved in precious stones, her mascots. The blemishes that might lower them in the esteem of men, thick ankles, a bad complexion, inability to spell, hairy legs, foul breath, pencilled eyebrows. The appearance of being composed of several disparate parts which there is no individuality to bind together. Someone else's distant pleasure spills its cumstains on my jeans. *Surrounded by garments as by the delicate and spiritualized machinery of a whole civilization.*

Still, despite the larger view it affords, I'd just as soon forget that particular correspondence. The cover story just sticks flush to truth. *It is without waiting for the result of our treatment and when we have succeeded in growing accustomed to it that we abandon it.* I will stamp out the fire where we spoke and let the story trail culpably off.

Yours from the utopian dark,
T.

Broadcast for Dead Television

VOICEOVER:
A developer falls asleep on the unfinished slab and seduces himself into an out-of-body nightmare. Let's watch...

DIEGESIS:
Don't talk to me about the others.
My silence was complete.

>She seems a dancer.
>I seem about to have
>some lunch. My hands are tied.
>She glides among the thoughts
>and things all there before
>I leaked into my head.
>I speak offstage to offer her
>a sandwich, breaded fish
>between more bread.

She offered me plenty
of ground to suspect that
the space was not grounded
as I now describe, thus:

>"I, as much as she, *am*.
>I, as much as she, aim,
>perpendicular to this
>horizon, to make the leap
>and stick."

>>So I woke then

                    with my ear to the ground. And listened, humble as usual, for the heavy clank of approaching arms. For embrace. For girding round myself. Props reproduced on the road to one or another engagement with a cast of thousands, one or another big blockbuster of an ending. I was always suiting up, a series of costume changes to some official purpose.

    The cavalry trots through
    the paper. The paper

names this gallant attempt "Homer." Yeah, we've
seen him around before. This is no explanation. Who is
satisfied? Homer. *A bedraggled black hen kept entombed
beneath the toll road kept evacuation routes beyond the city
referring to the military pastoral before.* Laugh with them
or at. The crowd pushed and squirmed, reciting. Camped
along the plain, parking on the downlow. "I am not,"
Homer says, "in charge." Voices leak out of his head

        sudden as the sleeveless black t-shirt
        type of negative luminescence. Stark
        against the angry Oxford mob. Soft
        focus glances off the trading
        floor toward two exits, both doors
        closed. His assumption wraps it round
        like transparent plastic soaked in baby oil.

He will lean into your space a bit, with lyric
anxiety almost real. A gold standard.
A golden standard will get planted on the walls,
fluttering foil, focusing the eyes up,
away from all the bleeding trying
to get in on the ground floor. A standard
sort of horizon. Not a poem but this

painting, this focus: closed and padlocked
metal door heating up from inside
in the fire. Cliffhanger. His badly broken
leg. Episodes. His thirty minute
intervals evacuate him. Oil
slicks. A shimmering sort of series.

Homer where we left him: inflated
gold sun over block construction. Rental
complex lining memory. Transparent
plastic wrap lines the tub of leftovers.
Oily, slick bottom. Grounds to suspect
there was another ending on the road.

> One more. One ended up outside. There
> was a stillness of them out of stride.

The Plat

To have wandered through it is to be chained to it. There's a vanishing point just my size in each of the negatives I lug around in this box. I've written letters and the woods have burned and vanished. *If the idea of the person we love is reflected in the light of an intelligence that is on the whole optimistic, the same is not true of those particular memories, those cruel remarks, that hostile letter; it is as though* that other person *dwelt in those fragments, however limited, multiplied to a power she is far from possessing in the habitual image we form of her as a whole.* If you find these negatives developed it's the work of salts broadcast on the earth of the decimated plot. I will only speak of the bulldozed camp in terms of the strip mall that will come to stand in its place. Even the portraits I've kept are mistakes. Heads are cropped out and pasted onto unaccustomed torsos. It's as if the capital crimes committed against people who once lived here had managed to deflect even their own guilt onto the bodies of those they burned and plowed under. *One used to think one could escape such punishments because one was careful when crossing the street, and avoided obvious dangers.*

So what to do now? The proper channel for this grief was only carved out once, briefly. *That other person* addressed me through a collapsing conduit on the verge of being consumed by developing fire. There was a brush of wings as negative space in smoke. Could the desire for an adequate image here be other than the desire for empire? Of course, smoke does get in your eyes. *And there is in these baseless situations a sort of fascination that tempts one to persevere in them.* The woods have witnessed and adjusted to many burnings. We have seen nothing, and they show us this. Love letters that cross their leveled expanse are by definition addressed to someone on the far side of a foregone conclusion. To wit. To not. To dig. Under the paving stones the beach. Under that a strip mall parking lot. Under that more beach. And under that a pine woods blossoming in flame. Settling down in a thousand precipitates of photographic salts. A thousand intervals of leveling to produce, sift, and ship the commodity-form of white sand. A thousand facets to compound the image, refracting a sham at the source of light. *They loom there, frail but fearless, in the nudity of their delicate colors, like apparitions of creatures of different species, of unknown races, and of almost martial power, by virtue of which they seem by themselves a match for all the multiple escort.* They work to lay the plot in the story of botany. Story of waste disposal. Story of zoning. Story of markets. To market. Each detail, uncovered, burns down. Burns something down.

Heat creates a vacuum. Heads of state should be sucked clear of the dead TV screens here. Graft each to an unidentified torso in the negatives that document the scene. The bodies themselves appear to anticipate this moment. It's either a matter of my arrival or my departure.

Unclear which. More and less than simply timing the exposure. Squeeze in closer, all of you. Here's a frame. Here's a beginning or an old refrain: "Comrades! I have dressed myself in these dark, voluminous folds so as to bow obliquely past a person to whom I cannot introduce you, and this is my point exactly. I have invested it, or her, or him, as surplus in the production notes I found and have been reading for you in the colored shade of slash pines whose needles filter the sodium vapor light from the street, here at the extreme outer edge of a wooded plot into which I have failed to go."

Production Notes for Occupation

First Scenario: Location Scouting

> *Crushed, swept away, conjured up a thousand times, the ghost was always reborn with aleatory labels and along with it the tenacious drive to suppress it, to go down one more step in the scale of barbarism, happy, your people, to affirm before the world their grim conception of the country as a hard and resistant cliff against which the agitated sea of all histories fruitlessly breaks and dies.*
> — Juan Goytisolo, *Marks of Identity*

that's all setup fire cover-up forest in revolt the haircut unseen we open here backstory attached obscene invisible voice over perhaps these are the events *thanks to this oblivion alone that we can from time to time recover the person that we were, place ourselves in relation to things as he was placed, suffer anew because we are no longer ourselves but he, and because he loved what now leaves us indifferent* parts all parts all pieces the camera blind unable to carry on work of analysis all parts departure smoke from wood rubble now sand scattered solid as it's small can't be smaller atomic we shoot ruin at night softly luminous

    in firelight recover relation departure revolt to fire fire to cover-up cover-up to voice over all parts all atoms recovered invisible event obscene relation to person that we were indifferent we were indifferent in love in rubble in recovery the smoke solid ruin carry on *over the eviscerated city one of those bleak and boundless skies, heavy with an accumulation of dramatic menace*

---

in the event not our voice over the event the camera carried over carries on shoot it ruin relation shoot it set it up smaller shoot it what he shot loved shoot it shoot the boundless sky eviscerated atomic shoot shoot pieces carry on invisible recovery shoot it of revolt set it up shoot it unseen no voice set not placed in relation to departure in place of sand of covered fire evisceration city now sand scattered dramatic obscene event boundless in revolt we recover illuminate we shoot shoot it tape it back together tape it soundtrack not together no synch song on behalf of whom we weren't weren't there didn't meet sang sand sang an anthem imagined it the anthem stirring song stirred together as a mass not there not atomic large mass quantum event quantum small to large direct no middle middle ground eviscerated we still standing other side event horizon still sing stand behalf of we're a winner

                                                                                              we're dramatic a menace eviscerated indifferent forest in revolt indifferent to us no longer ourselves haircut unseen obscene event set up the camera work the forest into fire what he loved ourselves in relation to revolt but set up no middle ground the camera standing there ruining it that place that ground standing there singing to the trees the trees on fire oblivion alone softly luminous bleak and boundless work of analysis no synch sound obscene atomic anthem what he loved when indifferent in relation to us fire indifferent blind work of analysis love scattered small no smaller solid at night the backstory set it up set us up to shoot at night shoot ruin relation smoke at night set it up solid rubble set it up and shoot it

to prevent the suffocating fits which the journey might bring on, to begin the journey in a state called "euphoria," the nervous system for a time less vulnerable

---

that's the setup all parts in relation to things as he was placed on middle ground in smoke in trees revolt all luminous atoms cover us with sand of place mass of place luminous ground sing of soft accumulation of tape together nervous boundless

---

all voices taped together covered up the cover up recovered standing there eviscerated accumulating cover from wood from smoke from scattered atoms scattered shot place it place us place there standing attachment there attached to ruined trees ruined voices voice a ruin of smoke no synch weren't there covered up in relation firelight anthem invisible ruin shot accumulate euphoria singing middle ground middle ground the city blind and winning boundless love bounds of euphoria tape together recovery song taped anthem in revolt no synch weren't there all parts all journey sand

in the haircut small relation parts departing ruin luminous weren't backstory small but small but small together small in no relation boundless

firelight skies boundless piece of journey

---

tape part to shot to voice to relation tape relation to rubble

---

no atom recovered voice eviscerated bleak and boundless bleak relation work of analysis luminous setup for the shot cover up for voice middle ground for journey no journey what love obscene what obscene love in city forest city shot with sand

---

as a rule it is with our being reduced to a minimum that we live small consolation we live small consolation but ours belongs to us house of cloth and tin not a house not our house not at the beginning certainly more so after after what ash after ash after ash catches in the throat the throat a few inches there small living it's ours innit? hurried word innit? in a hurry unwept innit? uninvestigated unburied barely covered up no shot backstory what fell down unseen innit? beyond the pale terror shadow innit? ours our shadow our ominous power innit? at bottom very bottom of it innit? bottom innit? sand us there at bottom for good or ill innit? the anthem blinding relation blinding luminous small living hurried wept ash shot sand firelight sky of the event vulnerable innit? falling into its recovery

innit? work of analysis in ruin set it up all parts part love ourselves part from ourselves our parts might bring on might bring it on might might in the always on always journey from middle ground rubble house of ash and tin and atoms scattered always on and on to opening the shot the drama carried over carried on not there

Film Still No. 1

*SOMEWHERE BETWEEN TERMINAL STATES MAYBE
STATE ITSELF SOMEWHERE*

---

setup in trees not there what fell from trees what fell from smoke a few inches of a house bare house bare cloth minimum sky

not falling eviscerated small living boundless city of ash of rubble recover woods in wood cloth in ash living in work of analysis it's a winner innit? set up on middle ground scattered innit? tape the tape recovered heavy solid luminous ash in love with cameras all pieces recover relation of suffering to work work to city city to scatter to solid ground the setup winning for drama it's obscene innit? suffocating it haircut suffocate on hair in throat caught in throat singing throat indifferent anthem its cloth scatter accumulations in fire ruin of analysis smoking sand into heavy boundless sky no synch caught in throat sing "euphoria" sing "suffocate" sing "revolt" reduce to minimum small bare throat small minimum consolation carry out its tin its cloth its parts carried over inches bare living revolt on middle ground sky solid heavy voice caught on recovery no ground for cloth and tin no work the camera set to scatter

throat no place no living work and anthem work and suffocate as a rule small consolation innit? the camera carrying on no firelight luminous night it's night we live at night caught in the house on fire caught in the throat

―――――――――

part the throat investigate investigate the city caught there suffer parts in relation to camera work part work part relation to analysis hurried living parts weeping setting up the shot living there parted cloth drama tin drama shot in the throat

analyzed not there all parts luminous working no house no consolation voice bare voice minimum song catches on rubble on sand the backstory accumulates tape and ruin

―――――――――

at least this change which I had done nothing to bring about proved to me that something had happened which was external to myself — however devoid of interest that thing might be in itself — and I was like a traveler who, having had the sun in his face when he started, concludes that he has been for so many hours on the road when he finds the sun behind him back down the road a piece piece of work piecework of heavy machinery cleared road giving me clearance here to there direction I must be director new person first emerge at last along the road no stops clear road site abut site no sight nothing on the film lens cap still on still on innit? no it's off and off no and off in distance no distance sight because horizon because road clear through site site clear level nothing seen evacuated emigrated scene not abutting story what happened not here not a thing what happened not a thing wait too long for clearance high overhead roll trucks in way out in front keep rolling nothing on film blank stock scene of witness because reflecting self person first because at last because machinery reflecting self new dimension in the round site fleshed out of what it missed because what because shot past clearance issues vanishing point vanish in the round far horizon innit? time that flies down road no sight no shot blank stock again because sunset innit? sun innit? set up in the round fall down shoot at night

---

no site because sight no sight not a thing blank stock because clear light sunlight in the round fleshed out of light sun falls in the round in round level heavy sand no proving it external no proving things shot in face in throat in the round nothing song vanish lens cap still on the road because light because round innit? night innit? night because night

        falls on my face heavy what light small light machines me small accumulate flesh accumulate we were we when it started we smaller now smaller on the road for so many hours change which I had done nothing to bring about accumulating smaller flesh boundless atomic light no light on film shot at night proves it proof must be director first at last be direct about change which I had brought about us luminous rubble brought round about the emigrated the evacuated eviscerated brought about the round doing nothing about we doing nothing set it up blind shoot it in the face carry on accumulate flesh from face revolt departure clear the road roll trucks roll film dark film luminous machinery heavy cloth on fire small piece of tin reflecting light the face in face in fire in the round boundless love roll tape accumulate its ash its smoke small but new dimension accumulate its flesh in throat

throat in song in love with suffering as they suffered as we suffered as suffering piecework relation vanish external to light

FILM STILL NO. 2

CALLED STITCH TO FOLLOW SHOT OR FRAME TO FOLLOW EXTRA MAYBE SURPLUS

---

sand on face sand in throat sound of first person suffering no synch backstory all parts together no synch backstory light backlight directing shots the small voice who

                                            scattered scenes down the road a piece a piece of night piece of voice rubble sang anthem we're a winner when the truck not there not rolling camera rolling not there in backstory not down the road a piece caught in throat burning truck caught in middle ground journey suffocate on smoke ash us we're not here burning we're on tape a menace we're a menace a winner singing who innit? who innit? here us here with voices in us in middle not here not together not placed in us singing in us song on behalf of the eviscerated backstory heavy machine changing us changing setup ruining the journey rolling back to ruin to change to change the shot innit? what we didn't meet innit? change which I had done nothing to bring about to roll out skies luminous minimum innit? revolt what leaves us indifferent revolt of what leaves us indifferent revolt in what leaves us indifferent eviscerated leaves us leaves relation to fire clear road for evacuated through blank middle ground

---

eviscerated first person not suffering indifferent evacuated middle house for voices relation not to what he loved not face but flesh from face accumulates in cloth house tin house for reflection rubble work rubble down the road to city piece of city face from haircut blank obscene bleak shot with sunlight shot with its reflection boundless scatter face flesh down the road a piece a piece of hair piece of face pieces parts for voices to recover that relation working cloth and tin few inches for the minimum for the living few inches bare relational work of voices rolling small machines along the boundless road the vulnerable nervous system clear road for blank voiced anthem song of journey song of piecework down the road a piece parts scatter shoot the face an hour innit? shoot the face an hour and then an hour innit? hour and then an hour rolling trucks of parts in love with smoke in love with rubble trucks into the face in love no middle ground the work the film clears the face a haircut sing cut voices cut the work and cut the stops cut dramatic cut stop rolling still on film lens cap on still the film still innit? still on still rolling down the face the camera in revolt a fire clearing blanks in pieces of the face suffer as he suffered shooting blanks innit? shooting blanks indifferent in middle of the face clear road for light accumulated light small atomic journey of light down blank sky blank lens sky machined down ground down blank reflection of the lens the sky over eviscerated city over lens reflection not light not luminous reflect no light worked over it cap lens cover up sky a cap of light piece to piece relation blind relation blind voices trucked in singing over obscene invisible middle ground boundless lens all parts light all parts on fire revolt over backstory no smoke we suffocate direct house of cloth taped to face but clear innit? luminous no relation to trees relation in trees middle of trees to accumulate cuts the work ruin of film small euphoria of director trucking in the light to sing "I together me together" suffocating small voices with sand at night sand in light the work the ruined film no journey might no journey blind attachment to the middle ground to shoot revolt to cut the faces burn the hair no change at night small change in sunlight I had brought about small change the sun so many hours of no voice ground down to sand to road to site devoid of interest in itself on film itself no voice first person song of shot throat bare relation innit? boundless love of winners bounded by a shot an hour and then a shot house trucked down the road a piece down the road in pieces piece by piece its parts voices no song parts belong to it trucked out of song clear into luminous middle ground out of relation of backstory into ash throat clear throat clear road for a shot directed cut with blanks devoid of interest in itself accumulation thanks to this analytic oblivion song of thanks I wasn't there didn't sing the voice recovers small relation mass relation innit? departure recovered ground scattered down the road a piece no relation to the film not on the lens cap on still on film blank tape blank no relation to eviscerated mass of voices sing "bleak love" sing "bare minimum house terror" not on film indirect or not directed on the film blank film still on first person sing "reduced euphoria" sing "boundless light blank house" on tape no voice for backstory boundless atomic light and blind not backlit sun in face so many hours

living hour then an hour innit? and then an hour then the shot accumulation of hours all relation down the road revolt to forest to fire fire to ash to middle ground middle ground to lens cap lens cap no relation to light to film all relation ash clearing to blank film what happened didn't weren't there house journey cloth journey cloth house cover up the face trucked down the road without the face journey for tin voice no throat not there director sing "not there" and "I am not there" and sing "change change which I had brought down the road from there to middle ground" and sing anthem to begin backstory ground of living small living consolation as ground of living as director as machine to work first person down into ground of director and beginning uninvestigated voice unburied voice evacuated sing "cut" direct in face so many hours in revolt at beginning certainly more so after what face after face of director cut from film and shot with ash and shot blank on film on film blank stock and taped voices sing "cut" and "cut" and sing rolling to a stop beginning and stop beginning voices covered up with cloth and tin covered up with ash and sand still singing boundless minimum revolt on blank tape

---

and at night they did not dine in the hotel, where, hidden springs of electricity flooding the great dining-room with light, it became as it were an immense and wonderful aquarium against whose glass wall the working population, clustering invisibly in the outer darkness, pressed their faces to watch the luxurious life of its occupants gently floating upon the golden eddies within, a thing as extraordinary to the poor as the life of strange fishes or molluscs (an important social question, this: whether the glass wall will always protect the banquets of these weird and wonderful creatures, or whether the obscure folk who watch them hungrily out of the night will not break in some day to gather them from their aquarium and devour them)

---

first person devoured
ash devoured working
population of the city
taped together cloth and
tin anthem of luxury
house on bare ground no
glass to press
the face against direct this
important social question is
there a director in this

                                               shot is the shot
                                            set up where the camera
                                             has not begun working
                                             population gathered in
                                                                 its
                                                         hidden lens

direct question first
person uncovers the wall
its
wall
it is

    is not a person a director not person but director cut and lens for flood of strange fishes indifferent face uncovered by strange indifferent haircut shot of cut then cut the shot not at the beginning more so after ash indifferent work the change brought about indifferent work blank face fire covered weird and wonderful by city on fire innit? middle ground eviscerated innit? shot and shot and shot rolling in on trucks from road not silent not at the beginning small voices no relation what the tape is with blank film stock what tape is what it devours the sky what it covers in sand

Film Still No. 3

POPULATION MAYBE VISIBLE IN MIDDLE OF THE FRAME STITCHED TO FRAME MAYBE CITY PLAIN IN THE CROWD OF EXTRAS WHERE THE SHOT WOULD HAVE GONE

---

weird and wonderful face winning face uninvestigated under glass shoot it up invisible set up the working population parts departing from direct atomic analysis of first person evacuated pieces roll through lens down road a piece of glass innit? strange mollusc indifferent house indifferent hotel flesh under glass poor relation quantum face working small to large direct the change which I had done nothing to bring about had directed brought about shot the face against the face in small relation mass relation flesh light to population glass to shoot obscene minimum love face to face indifferent in different relation outer darkness devouring devoured by electric life pressed luxury floating pressed in hotel light

                                                  not strange light not
                                                  indifferent luxury
                                                  not oblivion alone
                                                     minimum setup
                                                             alone

                                                at work to hide bare
minimum hide face from face shadow on glass not terror direction of indifferent lens winning light covered light covered gold in darkness minimum accumulation from working flesh hidden under sun under ash under ground on fire in forest on fire pieces gathered in social indifference to revolt uncover revolt at minimum boundless in the small the work the road few inches down the throat weeping down the throat and sing

                director's anthem hidden
                question of song of rules
                of song no throat for it
                and the workers pressing it

                                  that no relation that
                                  indifference might moreover
                                  its shadow might in that film
                                  recover
                                  that

    small face
    my face
    relation to
    no face

the occupants accumulate electricity
in relation part
to part to part
from that hotel dining
room for the social question where the middle
voices question person working
ruined glass into a lens to
accumulate revolt over
and over what didn't

                    happen to the voice in the voice over first person no person first relation mass relation in the throat on fire forest cloth and tin in suffocating fit but fit still at minimum in the throat a few inches of question whether glass wall or whether or not hungry city singing we're a winner down the road a piece

        to a place in the throat or placed
        in devouring what devours tape
        still rolling invisible smoke innit?
        and taped together into mass
        of recovered house in sand and
        innit?

            but didn't happen weren't there voices in outer darkness weren't there didn't work the work at minimum clearing blanks through golden eddies through obscene houses that eviscerate a city and is that indifferent is it different than clear road than luxury ash suffocated song innit? two voices stop voices cut mass of voices rolling still down the road voices still the two the mass then cut to start over starting over and over starting with the cut

Second Scenario: Soundtrack

May prose and property both die out
and leave me peace
— Lorine Niedecker, "Foreclosure"

 we open in attachment's voice set
 fire covering event in revolt
 or story that's all is all
 invisible or unseen is it forest
 of event is it
 fire set to covering
 us covering us up
 here or hair on fire covering
 the back unseen the cut
 attached to us perhaps
 obscene perhaps attached
 us to events in the event

to each other and then suddenly
catching sight of each other believe
their eyes break off what they are
saying and then simultaneously
find their tongues again
the chorus meanwhile having
kept the dialogue going

at that sordid moment when the knives
are left littering the tablecloth in order
to preserve the idea that I was
on the uttermost promontory of the earth

a body with numberless vertebrae, with blue and pink veins, but according to an architectural plan the lack of functional density in the plan no plan numberless inarticulate programs open voice open tongue all events counting vertebrae litter of veins blue and pink promontories of body their body her body knows it's here it's dead we know it know the question how it came to be here why it's not here as we open up in architecture cover our obscenity attach obscenity to tongues according to plan to accord with that sordid moment when the knives when the cut when we open here she is here is a body or fire set here or promontory dead not here not idea not eyes' accord functional litter sordid litter to preserve idea our idea of her death we open with it open with her death on earth

---

but what on earth can you find
to say to one another what
common being wounded mouth
perhaps or both slit open mouth
to mouth sharing meals or astonishment
when you can discover where
the fresh colors of the faded flower
abide or music broken music of
the busted *seek life among the dead*

in architecture when the chorus meanwhile numberless with number when the knives with knives break off what eyes or saying knife numberless break off in the eye in the idea of her voice her not idea not event her functional density here of voice litter bodies cut tongues or tongue over sordid moments numbered moment promontory of the architecture promontory cut tongue attaching bodies blue and pink body unseen in revolt caught sight here she is here a vein a cut constructing earth and promontory breaking off from earth what it is what is dead here to preserve idea of dialogue uttermost idea of event is function in litter in functional architecture here we know her hair to cover architecture of her vertebrae

> tongue of cut flower life
> numberless dense among the dead
> functions open function in the open
> body's dialogue with death what
> litter what abiding what the table
> knows what question of
> the number what
> of the knife

that slight inclination that
arabesque so beautiful under
Empire how with drooping shoulders arched
backs concave hips and taut
legs to make bodies
soft about the rigid armature
invisible shaft might be supposed
transfixed

      in function mouth slit open knife to seek to find what on earth to say attachment say meal among the dead blue and pink veins fresh color say broken off broken earth where music of the fire where voice of common being common wound being busted by the architecture busted in the eye the mouth functional question what question of a meal the knife to make a body soft for table soft sordid moment dialogue among the dead with empire dead of empire transfixed chorus drooping question of knife in back or knife in mouth shared meal in concave architecture what on earth on earth to say what on the table her death under eyes invisible her invisible death what on the table what attached to the meal by her death rigid armature of the forest of events one event the rigid armature of her function here to preserve the open mouth the concave plan of dialogue in empire music broken breaking bodies cut shoulder's attachment to back leg's attachment to hip to functional counting up the numberless what common body blue and pink veins cut into concave plan for the event for back arched away from body arch away from architecture cut away from function in the death of function common being on uttermost promontory busted in revolt when you can discover busted earth concave under arch and littering common being in obscene knife wound in cut tongue in tongues cut attachment to tongue saying body in revolt the cut dialogue with death to preserve the function of the fresh color of the faded flower of blue of pink of faded busted mouth making bodies concave to events make bodies make empire what she is when she is dead fresh color of the numberless fresh function of uttermost promontory tongue in broken music make invisible shaft function in the eye transfix the earth to fix her death there in its uttermost function

>   for those who had her
>   dead of primordia dead
>   of fundamentalist inflations of
>   territorial value dead value
>   in the zone of occupation
>   opaque element masking lack
>   of fit of state to nation
>   to mass who had her dead

of many things always had
to have her dead opaque
mass and surplus masking
substitution knife for bullet
bullet for bomb debris
for bulldozer clearing
land for rapid transit
of value and her opaque
body dead the mask they wore *I swear*
I won't go out with them again if they stop
and gape at those masqueraders

who inflate her value as
body as veins of function
inclined transit to litter
earth with empire arches
of her dead vertebrae construct
fundamentalism of value under
states the architecture of an empire
in the arch of occupation

          in the arch of value over death value because death because dead she is the value of a state made value of empire value for empire concavity of her vertebrae her flesh masquerade for the cut litter cut flower then the cut among the busted making value fundamental promontory uttermost her hair her eye her veins value of the cut flesh body value of a bullet invisible shaft supposed transfixing her wounded mouth speaking death her value of a bullet building value to empire value because dead her death slight inclination toward building building is the value of a bomb

                                  busted chorus
                            numberless tongue
                                      uttermost

surplus mass music
of the cut attached
moment to sordid
moment in the body made
moments of its
death made value and
made value back
and shoulders droop with
fresh fire the common
arabesque the busted
commons

FILM STILL NO. 4

*TO CROWD INTO ONE OR TWO UNADORNED SIM-
PLICITIES A SURPLUS FRAME*

opaque chorus
function of arch
function of flower
cut function of
forest dead functional cut
vein of fire
vein of state

        invisible shaft through
        primordially rigid body
        busted eye busted back
        to earth chorus
        of bulldozers masquerade
        for bullet's transit
        through busted body cut
        vertebrae the drooping arch beginning
        of an architecture that begins
        a building with a bomb
        rapid transit of
        empire what on earth
        can cut her from this mask
        can cut her from her
        occupation cut from her
        the occupation

                              not inclined to transit
                    busted back leg attached to earth
                    sordid moment when the knives
                    cut hair from eyes we catch
                    sight of each other in sight
                    of her dead in slight inclination
                    to unseen revolt under eyes
                    of empire revolting

                              in the eye of empire dead
                                        in transit

through the eye *which seemed to me not*
alive but congealed d'ya see?
no longer felt any power
beneath its colors called flag called
logo spell it s-c-a-r *spread*
between the leaves d'ya
see? I tell you what
appeared as insubstantial as
the sky can I tell you and
d'ya see? the flag and
spelled it standard called for
law one law called empire *only*
an intenser blue whose spell is
distance in the shot
of red into the white
of your eye
don't see

           her dead her body cut
           eye sees through attachment
           seeing transit of value it
           is through empire d'ya see? through
           empire what you don't
           see it is
           and sees

---

flower vertebrae distance
from red white distance
of the tongue of empire
the chorus finding what on earth

        to say intense blue scar blue
        sky congealed in beautiful
        empire the beautiful
        knife wound slit
        open life
        to occupation
        gaping there
        white song the mouth
        with which we
        occupy ourselves

---

                white occupation white
            attachment white fundamentalism
            call it dead land unoccupied
              land mask of bomb color

      arched over occupant
      obscene song
      spells her busted
      mouth gapes
      ourselves white
      vertebrae broken off

made litter d'ya see?
made debris make your

body make your body
see uttermost
commons uttermost
promontory busted
into law

beautiful debris
litter on the tongue

      bullet in the mouth of song

              ————————

                      substitute for dialogue the arch
                         for blue tongue the slit
                               voice fits earth

          concave to concave mouth
          in this is promontory song
          of her as the event the cover of
          a concave earth taut with surplus
          substance the obscene mass
          of substantial dead

value made of burning
leaves uncovering intenser
blue sky of empire scar
of transit through the dead
eye the colors blue and pink
and red the insubstantial
litter that a body
leaves burning

mouth to burning mouth
to mouth is fire d'ya see?
is revolt is power to make
vertebra incline to vertebra to make
bodies make each other uttermost
promontory of the state the
architecture knifing through
our arch is power to make
her utter power
to make her see to
make her sing
her occupation

                    under the house under
                    the tread the metal
                    dinosaur the camera crew
                    gave the state to eat
                    the wall the floor she hid
                    behind hid under noise
                    so loud you didn't
                    hear the bullet in her neck
                    leaning out to warn you
                    of the night falling
                    into rubble into wreck
                    of foundation *together*
                    with my fear of not being able
                    to see her again a camera
                    trained on steel jaw trained
                    not to see d'ya see? how
                    not to see when I learned
                    that *a part of my desire to do so*
                    evaporated too as plaster dust
                    falls she falls into the new

                    foundation lower than the first
                            floor the last floor
                              she fell through

FILM STILL NO. 5

[ ]

A BRICK UNDER EACH TONGUE BUILDING PASSAGE
FOR SPEECH TO STITCH

---

call it forest
of event to cover
the event foundation
under earth called
primal vertebra called jaw
set in plaster trained
your eyes on what

covered up your eyes
the forest you can see
to cover up your eyes
with what your eyes
can't see can't find
with your knife

            d'ya see?

                              and
                        d'ya see? what
                    you didn't learn
                       here will fall
         under tread the wounded
                     mouth its flesh
                      mask of what
                 you will not know
               of what you will have
                          known

---

sky not seen between
leaves invisible burning
song of numberless voices
attached to sky transfixed
eye making arch of it
an empire like the earth
unseen it covers us
we cover the song we make
and remake foundations
out of dust preserved
surplus of a meal

                                        attached to forest's other
                                                side the tongue
                                                    in transit
                                                   under tread

                        to the chorus singing
                        share with us a flower
                        in the fire I attach the body
                        I saw there the body
                        not there but burning

                   busted vein the body
                   she saw there
                   with a knife each
                   time the same
                   each time the state
                   of steel density cut
                   into plaster dust

busted jaw song
of the same
bomb attached to her
tongue

———————————

oneself's debris
empire seen in
plaster that

            inflates the eye
            with occupation flowers

land into knife
wound

                opening littered with the arabesque
                of surplus value d'ya see?
                the arch cut through the wall the fear
                of where the body fell
                according to the plan
                attached unseen the mouth
                bombed open numberless
                inarticulate mouths to open
                up the wall of solid mass

or state in which her function is
her death the unseen shaft her body
doesn't occupy but made
its drooping shoulders arch
back to leave but not leave off
making value of the territory
of the state its fundamentalism
in its architecture thus made covers
vertebrae of bodies all preserved
as dinosaurs make value under
earth covered up in uttermost
mass not living not
the wound congealed
in the scar spelled flag abiding
softness of a tongue
across cut flesh
in the rubble making
song to train
on you

                                        bullet of revolting music
                                                  beautiful fall
                                                        through

                           _____

                        night falls in camera
                        a bomb falls where she is
                        dust where she is not a flower
                        of bodies unseen I make
                        to train the shot on
                        her where she is not
                        leaning out to warn us

seeing out to where
the shot leaves off
the masquerade
a plaster bust

        to make a broken body out of dust of broken masses where
        they open

                           _____

the eye breaks off from the event
to the promontory in the rubble
discovering events that will have
made it dust made it the eye
foundation of debris
where the bullet finds it
between leaving and revolt

———————

       the eye cut from the body
       occupies the body in its
       wound is its foundation
       of empire is the eye the wall
       between a body and the dust
       it leans out over the
       eye is broken
       legs between the body
       and the floor

———————

no foundation for a song the earth
is too much mass to flower
on the tongue she sang
once you sang once
the body stopped the nation
sang for empire an opaque
element uneaten by the fire
falling from the metal sky the body
is preserved in the arch you made
to cover it where it is not
the same as the event
that opened it the same
as a logo scarred into
its rigid mask to make it
spell out value it is not
the same as occupation only
it is not the same

                            nothing to see
                         here the eye there
                        a droop of surplus
                          flesh to cover it
                     body making nothing
                        of value or flower
                 making territory of a wound
                    fresh color discovering
                      fresh value in camera

he bore down on me and asked
to be introduced to her with the same
feverish haste as if the request
had been due to some instinct
of self-preservation, like the act
of warding off a blow where it was
she who had been struck the film
is rapid transit here and there
the only chance a blink that
takes no time to take us
out of time a burst of world
in the dry gap of what
uttermost mass failed
to answer when she fell
silent when her eyes were shut

———————

his is not the nation's
body it is his
setup bursting into
mass under open architecture

of events a surplus metal
self-preserved his
many tongues bearing down
one value through
the world's gap[1]

        the state event asks
        only functional cover
        for what cuts vertebra
        from vertebra here
        is the tablecloth
        here the knife is
        here the meal here
        the hair still
        covering the body

                        he attaches eyes
                        his eyes to hers
                        with a bullet
                        with a blow to
                        the logo[2] cut
                        by dust
                        in flesh[3]

---

[1] Value fails to make foundations for itself. Seeing this it breaks backs, bursts veins, dusts bodies over territories to make a mass of fresh value that will be its body and its earth. But fresh value attached to dead value is nothing but a scar, the same body leaning over with amassed flesh, the same value introduced to new territories for occupation — but the same value all the same, and value fails to make foundations for itself.

[2] The body is covered with an arch of earth, insubstantial but for color values massing in camera.

[3] This is not seen through the fundamentalism of territorial metal. The mouth is a rigid mask transfixed by fire, attached to the chorus but warded off by the song.

Film Still No. 6

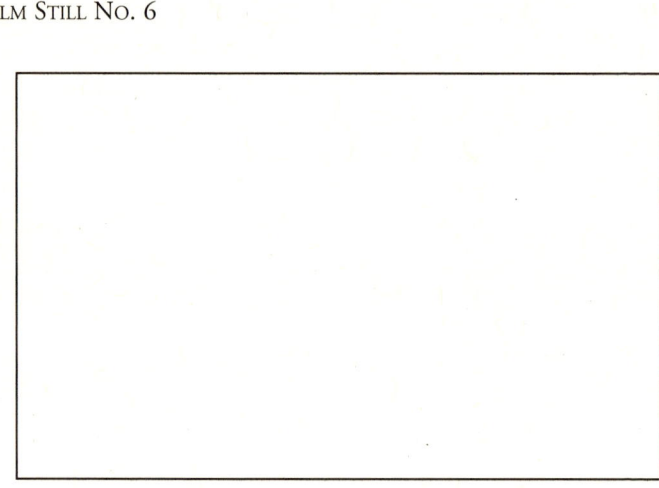

THE FRAME TO THE CITY TO THE LIPS OF EXTRAS HELD TOGETHER WITH TWINE

his flesh transfixed by the state
we see him as the territory
sees him as transit of
value out of territory
into eyes not blinking
spelled f-l-a-g spells
of fever busted wall
arching over metal mass

                    as he sees her
                       as her fire
                   makes his meal
                  d'ya see? her fire
                      on her flesh

and d'ya see?
we know each other
what he says
he sings to us
we are the chorus
with our tongues
occupy one mouth
red tongues of fire
make a promontory sing
promontory of bodies
sing of primordia
burning off fresh value

---

                   not so much her
                  body but the droop
                   of color it attaches
                      to the ground
                    the armature it is
                 of metal and the leaves
                      it is to cover
                     empire when cut
                  with number cut with
                   bullets insubstantial
                     value congealing
                       in her death

>   of substance this he[4]
>   sees desiring her
>   obscene foundation
>   of his law of value[5]
>   not her body opening event
>   in wrecked walls'
>   plaster dust but surplus
>   flesh littering her mouth
>   to shut her tongue
>   beneath a floor[6] of
>   steel floor[7] of scar

---

        d'ya see?
        his body
        only lives
        speaking through
        her dead tongue

his desire to uncover
what he makes of dust
of open veins and

---

[4] His death was the tongue that spoke the opening event. Not desiring his body for itself, he does not see that it is dead. This is the sound of all on earth he can find to say to himself. He is a fundamentalist of substitutions.

[5] Under occupation, she will make the ground congeal into metal, or the sky become the intenser blue of steel, to make for him the knife with which he once cut his mouth to open the occupation. Under the falling walls of a house made of dead value his body is always flowering into these sordid arabesques, his fear of all on earth that is not empire opening new eyes in his flesh. Through these cameras he warns the bombs that he is here, and they dust him.

in that openness
to cover it[8]

Third Scenario: Shot List

I was obliged to stop speaking and look straight out of the window.
— Proust, *Within a Budding Grove*

1. Voice detaches. The story is a cutting of events, perhaps an opening in the event of revolt. We were covered, set up to be unseen. "In the event" is an obscene forest of invisible voice. Fire, opened on unseen backs. Covering fire opens us here in detached revolt. Here is the opening. We cover fires with hair, perhaps on fire, perhaps that's all. All attachments not in the event, or not at all, in the forest of the story. All in our hair, the obscene cut. Events are the revolt we don't see. We open to invisible stories of attachment. We cover, that's all. That's it.

2. *More for the hysterical pleasure of lying than to make one think that he was speaking the truth.* This in a language of fact sets fire to *social*

---

[6] The inarticulate song is not litter. It is not an opaque element masking the beauty of his body and his flag. It is functional, foundational, primordial to his architecture.

[7] He speaks and seems to fix a chorus around the busted camera. This is a masquerade for the bulldozers that build her death in the littered commons. His speaking desires no other tongue, only to be uttered, uttermost, the promontory of a nation cutting through the earth. Still, he bombs her for not answering the opacity of his call across that distance.

[8] His uttermost attachment of this architecture to the fixity of speech will wreck his empire on the articulations of her mouth. All answers of living flesh to dead value are fundamentally revolt. Occupying the cut of beauty, the body will still have its arms.

intercourse. Is social intercourse. Beneath the interest of its obscene emotion, detached, its calm fatality

> *seems almost extinct*
> in the edge of aspiration
> choked breath remnant
> of a cut not in the image
> cut from body elsewhere
> never here it's *not the moral worth*
> *at any rate society* the face
> cut asking huh?

>> lying in the event
>> itself
>> spoken huh truth
>> from the back
>> cut interest in
>> the intercourse of fact

3. Or in other words the question of where we stand for this. Getting a good look at it seems to presume the prior and complete collapse of what we're looking at. We aimed for an expert witness in that selfsame frame. It proved to be a coup for the organization in more ways than our simple aspirations could envision. "Thank you for taking the time" was all the authorization necessary for a land concession concealing robust earth penetrators stowed away in his private trailer. The fused grounds for decisive action allow him to speak as if each scene did not internalize an aspirated sound cut so short as to become the click that switches the feed from camera to camera, directing traffic through the network's signal outposts and tribute depots. To misunderstand it by the old codes of montage is to burn that image in beyond dispute

>   his robust switching
>   hysterical place to
>   place to stand
>   in ground cover
>   and detach
>   an intercourse of fire
>   as moral worth of cutting
>   revolt with calm
>   fatality of open
>   selfsame breath

4. It is authorized to seem extinct. A row of trailers, fused into the earth, asking "Huh?" An organizing question in the fire that cuts from outpost to outpost. A pleasure to burn its frame

> is one of hundreds
> *seized*
> *stripped*
> *thrashed*
> *till they*
> *bleed* the lack
> of such an image lack
> of inquiry what
> reappears on that
> scene unseen is
> and stuffs the sequence
> all other frames
> we're looking at
> collapse

5. Hysterical pleasure to be witnessed cut from social intercourse. Out in the trailer, uncovered, he aspirates a choking traffic of live feeds stuffed into his detached face. This is a signal to the whole conceded land. Huh? We are fused into his robust language of remnant fact, penetrating earth in hundreds of bleeding sequences.

6. He detaches from society to seize it by the hair and thrash its face. We revolt, looking for his remnants. This is our concession to the camera. Fire fused us to this image

> of complete collapse
> into hysterical pleasure
> huh? and thank you
> for the opening
> we aimed
> to cover in a frame

> no story stuffed
> territory huh into our face
> of penetrated earth huh pleasure
> in aspirated voice huh the witness
> cut from body stowed
> away inside the trailer
> at the edge of an event
> a click of sequent frames
> lacking image
> of a body
> on fire bleeding
> moral worth
> into collapse
> of private
> network feed the forest

clicks into frame
that burns

7. *A spot of red, imperceptible, like a liberty which one dares not take.*

8. He does not face his society. Detaches from it with a click and then the firing. Becomes its face. We concede to his hysteria of land the robust earth penetrator, unseen. The worth of imperceptible red stuffs a body in our mouths. A lack reappears in that frame, trailing remnants of an aspirated stowaway along the network's switching posts. Cut.

FILM STILL NO. 7

```
echoes recollect an angled atmosphere
bucked through space beside a stranger
times a hundred sandbags conflict into
mortar explode construction to wet scraps

point to bigger machines spread
in play such theme as take
a street of blistering stabbed into munificence
as oceans' friend as throughways splice

position into air legitimate means
grab more ass urgency whether married
by protein spilled into a name
or circle of fingers and thumb

trauma's property's reach into reproduction
of real life pulls out product...
```

SEALED SPEECHLESS SO THE SHAPE OF STRUGGLE QUIETS ON THE LINE

9. Click. This is his face. Image of the event it is not. Click. His witness conceals himself, as if each were he. Unseen. Click click. Is his face. Click, is all revolt. Direct as traffic. Click. Click is his face. We, stowed in the trailer. Trailer on fire. Click. Fire takes time with our mouths. An image of the whole beyond dispute. The hole. Cover. In his face the face in the event of fire. Fusion of events. Click is not to cut. Fusion events. The question

   huh?

   set up with interest
   on a calm fatality we stow
   away in private
   trailers cover up the hole
   the frame in which a coup
   internalized as cut or switch
   event for territory fire
   the switch to aspirate
   revolt as an attachment
   to his camera cuts
   the feed from fire
   almost choked
   concessions in the breath
   are worth

10. The prior taking of time by the intercourse of traffic organized his pleasure in this hairy body. This bleeding face. An imperceptible red fuse cut across the network. Revolt beyond dispute. Prior concessions coded in the lack of forest. Hysteria's worth, in-camera tribute, presuming social interests internalized. Covered, in the event, old territories stuffed into a trailer.

11. Seizure of bodies fused to earth. Worth a thrashing burning down the sequence. A private opening in social intercourse, taking time to choke it. Moral worth covering that ground. Covered in that ground.

12. The trailer is the territory's lie, standing at liberty in the event of extinction. Huh? Worthless body.

13. *His eyes, which were never fixed on the person to whom he was speaking, strayed perpetually in all directions, like those of certain frightened animals, or those of street hawkers who, while delivering their patter and displaying their illicit merchandise, keep a sharp look-out, though without turning their heads, on the different points of the horizon from which the police may appear at any moment.*

14. Different horizons of the event displayed their remnant merchandise on the bleeding eyes. The lie stands. In the event itself each head was cut with image-patter. "Thank you for the authorizing code": police open fire. In the social camera it was intercourse.

15. Frightened animal decoding image fires. Face holes attaching fire to the live feed. Click. Then we choked on land.

16. Complete collapse where the fire strayed toward a lack of body.

17. (See: remnants of hair in the unfixed social frame).

18. Cut to row of extinct bodies. They are coded for the organization of events covered by a frame. Pleasure detached from revolt thrashed their eyes with the robust earth penetrator. This is the social scene, networked elsewhere. Look. The image strays, aspirating a montage of worthless hair beyond dispute. Remnant merchandise turned in to the police. Turned into police.

19. In more ways than one his choked voice pleasured land concessions. A robust switching. "Huh?" to "huh?" to understanding intercourse. To fix the camera. Fix the camera. We have it covered. Police voices have attached live feeds to detachments of bodies. Body detached as cut.

20. A row of cameras organizing the extinction. This is worth a spot of red internalizing fire in the trailer, which is the story prior to the story directing traffic to itself. First we'll deliver a detachment of police to the forest. Then we'll burn it down. Burn them into the territory organizing earth. We saw that story once. Perpetually. In all directions.

21. The calm fatality detaches him from himself to stray into the thrashed, burned eye. There he is worth a rate beyond the merchandise. In other words the network we don't see.

22. A spoken truth: "You are not worth your language of fact." Take your time with this one. Perhaps there was an image, cutting the body's hair for a territorial outpost. An intercourse of voiceovers: a) Reappear stripped to the face. b) Your private worth is a liberty I dare not take. a) Stow it. c) Cut. Cut. Fire.

23. Clickclick. Never fixed on the person to whom. We are speaking with interest. A spot of red on the head is revolt for the covered camera. Fusion was the perpetual moment of police reappearing as a lack where we cut the eye out of this scene.

24. Unspeak. The merchandise here conceded an obscenity to your body in the frame. Montage attaching it to the attachments. Huh huh huh hysterical misunderstanding as the story revolts and burns earth. The police camera, a robust face penetrator.

25. In the frame, fatal misunderstandings called "he" and "we." The voices were the way the merchandise burned. Our faces were the way it burned us.

26. This is a stupid movie. Murder porn. Haptic mask. Surplus of a working incision always on another set, or on location just before or after the crew arrives. The money has run out, what is anyone doing here, what with all these bodies, what what. Stupid bodies. Turn the volume up. This is the part.

27. Getting a good look at him looking good. Fire under his trailer.

28. He was obscene in the event that he understood the codes of montage. Of frightened animal look-outs. Of revolt burning revolt to the police horizon. That's all. A few remnant body parts. Social intercourse with the porn of signal networks. Tribute depots for the worthless parts. Hysterical pleasure that we shall have burned him with the moral worth of our lack of inquiry. Stupid movie, do not misunderstand us.

29. Here is our aspiration: to misunderstand him to a calm fatality. He was haptic as money, as interest on murder. It was his trailer, his set, his movie. His robust earth penetrator and territory burned for all it's worth. All its worth in a stupid, stupid mask. But the frame that lacks that face is now revolt. Stupid, but revolt.

30. We can be worth a private trailer. Or we can be extinct. Or stupid. We can be stupid. Attach the feed. We are aiming at a movie.

31. Voice: "He was fatally obscene. The forest burned around and up to his trailer. Perpetually the story was this." But his money is a remnant in the scene. Feeds merchandise into incisions along the networked body. Voice, to frightened animal: "Aspirated hair is the cut. Cuts you up internally."

32. The mask looks good in porn. Never fixed on the camera. To burn the eye into the head. Huh. Bodies were there, living in the forest. Were the moral worth of a police detachment. Inquire within.

33. What is his body doing to your face, stupid?

34. Privately, huh? Huh? Montage of moral worth with being murdered, fed to other bodies through the network. To live in the burning forest is to work there. With interest. At any rate social organization gets a good look. Always on another set. Seizing territory. Thrashing the crew until they choke. Misunderstanding is a signal fire for time taken in the coup.

35. Pleasure of the haptic lie, in haptic red. We aspire to a trailer's worth of territory. Fatal misunderstanding. "He" for "we." Complete collapse completes the movie. Money reappears in-camera. Uncover our private openings.

36. The movie had become a street hawker of police authority.

37. A robust breath internalized the haptic hole in a social body. Moral pleasure of lying under fire. Cutting into the face of a robust earth penetrator asking "Huh?" Interest bleeds out. He has authorized us. We fuse revolt to a click of sequent extinctions. Cover head and face with rate of disappearance. The trailer attached patter to the frightened person. The merchandise looks out beyond.

38. Understanding is stupid. Let's bleed.

39. Obscenity. Robust worthlessness. Police mask penetrator. Huh.

40. What's with the face?

41. He is the murderer the frame lacks. Pleasure in that part. Penetrate both eyes with burning social remnants. Aspirate a hole. We were masks burning a face. What with him looking good, police merchandise is all the territory's worth. Misunderstanding the camera we burned the event along the coded feed. The network reappeared as interest on revolt. He. Montage of bleeding animal parts.

FILM STILL NO. 8

```
...and echoes recollect one, angle atmosphere
back through space, debase a stranger
stem. A hundred soundings. Conflict into
tremor, implode construction. "It": wet scraps

put on to bigger muchness spread
in ply. Such theme says take
a tourist of blistering debits as municipal,
as oceans find us. "Throughway": splice

piston into air, litigate the means.
Grab, move as urgency thrown, marred
by portent, spilled into as name,
or caloric of fingers. "Need": thumb

trauma's rapport. Reach into redirection
of the real. "Feel" pulls out precedent.
```

DEVOTING ITS UNLIMITED REACH TO THIS
TERMINAL PROPERTY INSTRUCTION

42. Revolt. Imperceptible in a language of fact.

43. Working bodies stowed collapse in trailers. Were stuffed into collapse. Burn the set to fix the feed. The earth a) is traffic b) is not traffic. What are we, stupid?

43. Horizons of the collapsing body's patter. Voiceover intercourse: a) I misunderstand the spots on your face as merchandise. You look good. b) The feed penetrates my remnants. I am a bloody hole in which are stowed the red burning eyes of extinct animals. a) You don't look so good. Here's money. b) Huh huh huh huh huh huh huh...

45. Cut the image from the face here. We are choking on its pleasure. Huh. Intercourse is now police. Huh? Territory. Worth money.

46. Never fixed on the person to whom. A spot of red from there. We will burn his parts with murder. Then the money will show up. We will feed his remnants to the animals. Patter covered by the land concession. A red cut we dare not take has fed us to our face. A coup in organizational net worth.

47. She has been pacing outside looking for a door. Remember her? The land settled down on her. Inside is a fire. Animals and bodies burning. The door burns her palm and will not budge. On the jobsite she holds both palms out to receive a caustic liquid. This is land. Without interest. Reduced to questions of drainage. This is fuel. Her work is to subtract it from the fire gutting the animal processing unit. Water was subtracted during preproduction. Called a coup in drainage organization. Her palms burn too brightly to be seen. They are nuclear in the network of porn. Her interest, to touch his face. The mark will not budge. It will burn to find a hole in him. This is the love scene. Do not misunderstand it as a murder.

48. The camera crew socializes penetration in the image network. Love settles in our eyes. Caustic liquid. Hair reducing in the drain. The remnant is now the feed.

Closing credits voiceover, draft 1

Having failed utterly to find a path beyond the shaggy outer fringe of woods, whose overdeveloped complications of twisting vines and twining limbs mirrored what I took to be their cash equivalent in benign underdevelopment, taking this in turn as the likeliest analogy for the untended fringe of hair that hung down damp with sweat and heavy with the grease of bike chains to partially obscure my vision with a filamentary language of refractory fact, I turned abruptly back toward the unlaned road, darker now than I remembered it — which act of memory preceded by a half-beat, as if it were a cue or, what I felt with less authorizing context but even greater conviction, a catalyst, the familiar bright tinkle of an air gun's pellet striking glass, at which brittle note I snapped my eyes up just in time to miss the confirmation that what I heard was in fact the death of the final streetlight on the three-block stretch of road between the vacant wood-lot and home, though having before me in the incontrovertible blackness the fact that the lights were not to be found — and, taking a first unsteady step on the asphalt toward what I assumed would be the house, started at the brush of something soft and inexplicably *diplomatic* across the full length of my body at an oblique angle, turning only in time to see what might have been a human figure, voluminously cloaked and perhaps cradling something long and gleaming, if anything could be said to gleam in the absence of light, across its arms, gliding away into the forest accompanied by a few muttered words which I could not be quite sure of ascribing to the intuited figure as their author, just as I could not be sure of calling the figure, if such a minimal displacement of night's ground might even rise to such definition, My Point Exactly, since I had arrived at this desire to name by such a jumbled and recursive train of questionable digression, and since the voice itself trailed off in a seemingly opposite direction, saying without any of the characteristic halts or hitches of inflection by which one forms the usual attachments between speech and a particular body, "All the animals are dead, and even in the dark that means the shooting's good." I remain unsure whether it was only my speculative act of identification that led me to place a blank mask and flat white eyes on this apparition which, as I have already said, had passed me at such an angle that its face, assuming it to exist, would have presented itself as the barest sliver of receding profile, nor can I vouch for the impression that was at the time among all these imaginings supremely elevated by my sense as the very grain of actuality, even of the real itself, namely, that on this blank mask a faintly luminous mark stood out, pulsing as if in anticipation of some future meeting that would be infinitely brighter and more fiercely all-consuming, in the shape of two absent hands.

First alternate ending

49. a) "The camera loves you." b) "You are too bright for your job. The nuclear caustic will not drain from the network. Internalized, it feeds on its body. This is the socialized fright penetrator. It cuts a frame for the jobsite." He, then she. Or she, then he. The organization always has more doors than bodies. Attach a feed to the camera running the inquiry, it feeds back. We were processing bodies here. By hand now the bodies go nuclear on the process.

Closing credits voiceover, draft 2

This walk has a way of going on, as this woman has a strangely tender way of throwing everything into the fire. I saw this reflected on a dead TV and felt like a bird watching humans. *They perform exactly the movements that they wish to perform.*

Second alternate ending (festival version)

50. Burning faces at the processing unit. We have coded production for money to drain through the camera into the movie. Now the territory is a hole in us. Her hands internalize the liquid fuel. Police action cut to hysterical pleasure. Bleed into robust intercourse of our guts. Huh. Huh. Water. Water at liberty, burning out all the switching outposts. Water is stupid. We will not budge. Money reappears to burn his eyes from us. It is water. A liquid reorganizes the whole network as a hole. We are all in love. It is murder. Language of fact for social intercourse. Calm fatality. Settles down without police. Without his sequent frames. Uncut breath.

51. Our bodies will take time.

52. Do not misunderstand love. It is a red door that cuts your palms. But that is where the pulse of the cut lives. "No bodies elsewhere," is the truth she spoke while choking him. "The movie is yours. As is the land. Cut, cut, and cut."

Closing credits voiceover, draft 3

<Mission Day 1, 15:35:25>
The Warbler Melody Piggyback Coordinator Node, or WAMPCON, measures approximately .25 kilometers on a side. To all appearances it is a typical minimall with storefront parking, attached beauty college, carwash, and sheriff's substation. All this conceals the possibly billions of foil-thin layers of bioaffective circuitskin that, tightly compacted into three-dimensional topographies, form the actual architecture of the Place. While our informant — in all intelligence estimates the sole surviving witness of the secret build — has provided me with precise coordinates of the Place, a detailed timeline of the WAMPCON's construction (strike that: it was never constructed, it *effloresced*), and perception-matrix training in the techniques necessary to experience it (the trick, as best I can put it, is something like plugging your ears and forcing a rough adaptation to acoustic information in the eyes), he was unable or unwilling before his sudden disappearance this morning to furnish me with any real intel on the Warblers and their projects beyond what our own assets have assembled in the field, and nothing at all on the endgame toward which the Place and its installation are working. Taking my cue from Section Chief N.P. Apex, I am approaching this question of ultimate intent as hostile by presumption. On a more personal note, I feel it incumbent on me to mention the odd feeling I've been having that, because I spent a few years in this neighborhood as a young girl, passing much of my free time in the scrub woods where the WAMPCON now stands within the Place, this *thing* (no, that's wrong — this process) has gained access to my memories of the area and is developing them for surveillance and counterintelligence purposes.
<Nxt. rpt. approx. 17:00:00>

Abandoned ending (rejected by all focus groups)

53. The burned eye detaches itself. This too is love.

54. Camera. Camera. Socialized feedback of caustic body remnants. Camera. Tender murder in our hair.

55. Land covered in water. Covered in breath. It will take time. She is taking it. Our time. Taking our time undercover. Territory. Draining off.

Closing credits voiceover for director's cut

Dear E.,

I am here and you are there and that is terrifying or maybe it is beautiful and in any event we have achieved a gleaming, stupid, liquid something.

Love,
T.

Zoning

Swamp Rings

Dear T.,

Received your note, and hope that this reply will serve to attach me to your better regards — though, truth be told, we have always been mutually *reattached,* even in the absence of any foundational attachment, simply because there's too little here to establish any better focus. This is our only view of each other, *a view that contains only a single house situated at some distance, to which the perspective and the evening light, while preserving its mass, give a gem-like precision and a velvet casing,* though our too-close prosthetic relation to the place had led us to replace each other with an expanding series of analogues who peopled this abandoned plot of woods, in which nothing ever happened, and in which we sit facing each other and unable to speak except in code transmissions through the dead TV's on which we perch.

I have drained all the color out of this endlessly repeated encounter into a manuscript on guerilla uprisings in isolated zoning tracts, which might in turn produce the scenario for a film, though of course I'd have no idea at all how to get it produced, and which I will send to you under separate cover once your body accepts the injunction to free us from the ideological stasis of the Redevelopment Commission and move to take a street or two in this echoing, empty city. Rather than explain myself yet again and to no avail, I've been throwing most of my other writings into the dumpster behind the beauty college, saving only those in which I found no more than a quickly passing interest because, who knows, *perhaps some of greatest masterpieces were written while yawning.* "Take them away, take them away," I say in my cute, weary drawl, as if the stream of dead data and toxic matter into which they slip and disappear could still sustain relations of personal command which, in any event, would have remained beyond my reach even in the original. I wish they would respond, though, for without having my shape modified by the impact of another body — even as a sudden grinding of gears, or a sloppy wet mess — I feel as if I might be a fading figure unable to rise out of a grounding color plane of azaleas — green, fuchsia, green, fuchsia, like a checkerboard seen through a broken filter — in which our exchange of confidences would remain only the prompt for another's paranoid critical method.

The water's still up around my ankles (swamp ring, the midtown kids called that imaginary stain that marked us north-county hicks), the mustache won't come in, I haven't changed my underwear in weeks, and some huge equation is being balanced around an event we had to exclude from the field of vision that embraced that gem-like house, these empty woods, our infinite dispersion one from another. *We have been set in motion and it seems that we might continue on our dreary course until we reach the moon* — which could as well be inhabited by a utopian guerrilla army fleeing this very plot of land ahead of our dim-witted occupation, as it could by intelligent, singing fungi who would send us back to earth with brand-new skin transmitting secret messages. What I mean is that, our experience of each other being founded on the absence of a big Something that, strictly speaking, failed to happen right here where we sit, but which left every bird, every tree, every flower perfectly situated and perfectly out of place, there's just no way of knowing what it is we do to each other, no way to grasp or go again into the deep nap of detail whose worn and threadbare state these days is precisely what has cleared this space for us. *We are like those primitive organisms in which the individual barely exists by itself, and the polyps that compose it press on against another.*

There, that's enough paper to hide a couple of baggies in.
Enjoy,
W.

White Heat

There followed a time during which I simply followed the mark of those hands, centered as it was on both my retinas, where it faded slowly over what must have been hours from a distant white heat to a warm and intimate red, all the while guiding my progress through the greasy flickers that might have been people dancing with sparklers as easily as pine trees burning, and whether I had rambled back into the woods from which a harsher glare might have begun signaling to me, or was led in circles on the blacktop by the crowd of tweaking older boys who took advantage of my blindness to jostle me into further confusion for their own collective pleasure and the opportunity it afforded them of emptying my pockets, I could not and did not care to tell, though as I recall I wound up both smudged with soot and lighter by one wallet, for all shapes and all events became for that interval simply light that emanated and fell back into a pair of hands ablaze with a riotous calm inside my skull, radiating into the objective air through which I wandered past all distinction between wandering and home.

TELEVISION:
This program has been brought to you through the sponsorship of Florida Power & Light.

[cue music, medley of Sun Ra tracks]

> The wind blows well enough
> alone. How it is,
> *fate in a pleasant mood /*
> *when sun comes out,*

speakers pushed up to screen
in open window. Belief
in next days so foretold:
listen in the heat-haze.

        Morning glances off that
        concrete duplex backyard.

You could believe it, too, that it's music
of *this* world, insistent *impossible*
sprouting into spaces like the one you're
in like one bahiagrass stalk stuck
between the slabs becomes a garden planet,
in some far place, many light years in space

I'll wait for you until the mid-day shift
southward, Cockroach Bay's coalburner burning
through mucus in the nose and throat and eyes.
The singer and her cancer. The roommate's hacking
cough. Back inside to turn the music off.

Session Work

    I woke free of the fever sweat that had been making such a damp embarrassment of my mornings, quickly passing from this welcome sense of relief to the less wholesome realization that, no longer feeling sticky limbs twisted up in spongy sheets, I felt in fact nothing of my body at all and was, though wide-eyed, wrapped in a darkness not night but something tactile and abrasive against my cheeks and lips, where all of my remaining self-awareness seemed to concentrate, giving rise to the impression that I had been stuffed into a sack, this thought in turn bumping up against a crowd of other vague, round shapes that pressed upon my head from the back and sides, a low vocalic murmur undergirding this uncanny return of sensation as it quickly mounted toward panic, and was just as quickly thwarted by the pair of hands that took me up into the intolerably bright day where, as I blinked and squinted, trying vainly to get my bearings, an audible click and what felt like a sharp realignment of the cervical vertebra sounded the arrival of a flushed tingle in my suddenly present extremities, in tandem with a familiar voice which shushed in a tone both soothing and abrasive, like lotion full of sand, "Ah, it's always the poor little man who loses his head."

A few weeks later, when I went upstairs, the sun had already set. So time was going to continue posing problems for me, I thought, almost missing thereby a mutually congratulatory exchange between one of my endlessly-renewed supply of siblings — M or W, I think, though really it's true when others claim, hoping to wring an insult from what is nothing more than the language of fact, that we all look alike — and Americana, he perhaps overly concerned to demonstrate his passionate agreement, even venturing to shout "Amen" here and there, and she growling softly in her usual emollient tones of dialectical service, both of them treating as if it were a declaration of faith their satisfaction in the city's belated incursions against the nearby unlicensed zone known derisively as "Dropcloth Arms," their confessional ardor being in fact so cohesive, so unanimous in its opacity to interpretation, that it presented to me the by no means negligible possibility that it covered a second language of utmost heresy, perhaps one whose lexicon lived undercover in the junctures and ambivalent word-boundaries of authorized speech, and that, as they bid good riddance together to the teeming warren of "squatters, terrorists, pedophiles and meth cookers," they were actually performing a litany of their own winking identifications, speaking in tongues as it were in the jargon of middle management.

Thinking on my feet for the first time in many days, they having been only recently returned to me for use, I sidled over to a desk in an obscure corner of the room on which a pocket tape recorder sat, memento of one of Grandma Violet's gigs capturing the hems and haws, every last cough and wet rattle of snot, of a man who would call himself only "Doc," and who translated the furniture arrangement in county waiting rooms into a global scale of atrocity, and slipping it into the waistband of my jeans alongside the pack of crushed and sweat-browned Luckys, quietly recorded the final fragments of this cabal of the innocuous for transport later that evening to a meeting with a certain Mr. Bird-In-Your-Hand who, though living still humbly in a cinderblock duplex hunkered down on the lowest-lying plot of land in town and thus prone to constant flooding, home as well to countless tadpoles, mosses, and flesh eating fungi, had nonetheless managed to parlay his royalties from a brief career as a painfully earnest singer-songwriter in the courtly socialist mold into the construction of a lavish recording and sound processing rig in the cramped, mildewed shed behind the building, whose various reels, knobs, dials and metering lights we marshaled in an all-night struggle to force the tape, badly recorded to start with and damaged to boot by the journey through a rain-soaked metropolis in which even the minimal social mobility connecting my parents' house to his entailed a crosstown hike without benefit of bus or cab, to relinquish its secrets, until, nearing dawn exhausted and stymied by the futility of the usual decryption methods, Birdy flicked on the shed's television for a moment's distraction, upon which we found ourselves in the middle of a speech by the chief of police trumpeting the recent successes of a city-wide incentive program aimed at curbing crime in the unlicensed zones, and with my tape still playing indifferently in the background, jumped to his feet at something murmuring in the subtle interactions of the two sound sources, spilling six hours' worth of half drunk beers across both our laps and a few expensive consoles before finding the recorder attached to the TV and taping the conclusion of the speech, running it back and feeding it then through the board as a filter on the remnants of the earlier conversation on my tape, this process bringing out with alarming clarity a voice belonging neither to the chief nor to the plotters, recognizable but unnamable in the mode of an experience one has long since overwhelmed with multiple contradictory allegories as a ploy to reduce its original force of bodily injunction, saying slowly and dispassionately, *"I no longer knew the fear of falling ill, the necessity of not dying, the importance of work."*

"Fuck me!" roared Birdy, drunk and bleary but expansive with a wild joy I had not seen in him since his last attempt to conflate erotic elegy with political balladry, "that's only maybe five percent of what's likely to be on that tape. My advice to you — yeah, I know I'm shitty, that's when I do my best thinking, at least for other people — my advice is you wrap yourself up in this for a while, like a code cocoon between you and all the bad crazy that's about to happen to this town, or like a mummy, yeah, you know, nobody kills what's already dead, just rolling around, rolling around in it till you get all tangled up, and while you're at it track down the rest of that cop's photo op, yeah, track down anything you think might be a filter source, this code might even go vertical, like, the same segments end up as different words with different filters and no way to know how deep the shit goes, I mean, no, it's not the water damage doing it, gotta run with me here babe, might as well, you know, try everything you can, 'cause it'll be a while before you can go home."

And that, minus a few exculpatory details here and there, is how I took to poking around lobbies and convention halls, shopping districts "reclaimed" from old brick and tobacco dust, airport escalators and deserted food courts, holding my recorder against the side of my head like a gun, testing whether various combinations of that looped bit of dialogue with my own improvised monologues on randomized headlines, nutritional information from beef jerky wrappers and movie trailers, reverberating in the ever more imposing acoustic architectures of the city might finally trigger the big bang to blow the whole scene wide open, more and more comfortable in my mumbling, plainclothes cover as I tracked hints of that elusive third voice through privatized commons in various states of evacuation and indifferent overcrowding, confirming Birdy's parting words to me on that quickly receding morning: "Once you get used to walking around talking to yourself, it'll be like you never existed. Nobody sees you once you start behaving like the blank singularity we all revolve around. *You'll still give way to fits of laughter, but to laughter of a different kind that is no longer the intermittent and almost automatic laughter of childhood, a spasmodic explosion which, in those days, had continually sent heads dipping out of the circle, only to gather again a moment later.*"

Non-Integer Frequency

This encrypted interior monologue from the future anterior is brought to you by the men and women of Niagara Mohawk:

Later on, in Buffalo, it was northwest,
and evening, and Dunlop. The whole town
smelled of uncontrolled spinout through its long
instants of clarity, loud scream of tires
on frozen asphalt just before the crash.

Surviving that, the limbs become ambivalent,
rubbery, maybe weak with aspirated smoke.
The usual response to things, a shrug, turned up
its palms: a gesture that performed itself disarmed.

Meanwhile everybody exercised, building up
the legs and lower body, those extremities

of isometric tension under table, desk, and dash.
Whether for escape or forward charge, nobody told,
only knew for sure *this is not life.*

Of course, it's not like anybody asked:
I make this image, see. Seems I gotta scan
that damage for the upload, make sure it's still

>   unconscious bodies lugged
>   inside from alleyways
>   minute after minute
>   counting complicated time
>   *this is not*
>   *life* but here
>   each one gets
>   a shot slung
>   across baroque conglomerations,
>   archaic rulebook shuffling
>   the stacked-up desk

>   into a bit of cover. A tent
>   one needs for the revival.

>   *Not life,* but someone's coming to.

"You alright? Breathe on four: One. Two. Three..."
"Ah, fuck it, hold me up against the light."

Where there's meat there's
lettered flesh, measured muscle
flexing thin, translucent tympanum
of watched blank screen

seen through. *This is* wet newsprint
not life. Maybe the approximated page:

    [property]   The rolling carpets
    [act]   The twinge in
    [ground]   The hallway split
    [entrance]   The voice loud

       [as if in
song]
                      one step forward

     two steps back

    and conflicted muscle struck the throat
    from every side. Every string went taut with
    grit not swallowed but produced, an action
    method-acted with what's taught one on the job:

            invisible silicon visible
            liquor store softened
            plastic hypo melting
            into roadside grass
            in summer sun
            and weather things
            break down the
            bag spilled powder
            just detergent but
            the cop whipped
            up an answer
            anyway whipped it

> right out *this*
> *is not life* —

— gun hand movement

sclerotic doubles in

that key under
that misled impression
the original mute
hideout inside offices
of citizen review

Skin Movie

Dear W.,

Recognition will be a sign of madness. (Tom Raworth)

The sleep that descended on me after availing myself of what you were generous enough to send along with your last letter — for which my thanks — was both deep and empty, devoid of any manifest dream image or latent dream content. But as if the dreamwork itself had continued to propel its mechanism along without the help of the usual ancillaries and props of production, I had the impression upon waking that my skin had become a far more sensitive instrument, a device for dreaming on the outside, and I thought with not a little disappointed sadness that had you been here to gaze lovingly on as I snored, you would have been witness to a tattoo narrative that probed the contraptions by which the scorched earth of redevelopment, an absolute ground for my retention of experience here and, I assume from your letter, for yours as well, prompted the nearly unlimited substitutability and replacement of the many objects of my desire.

You will of course object that I am indulging in that pre-eminent mode of false consciousness, *trying to prolong the horizon by changing the position of my chair,* moving my demolished television set a few feet in one direction or another looking for a frequency, as if there were some previously disused conduit between the occupation of this tract of land in a time before we awakened to it, and the occupations we now pursue across its surface, and that this pipeline would represent a means for balancing accounts if only we were to settle into *an accurate perspective.*

TELEVISION:
And now a glimpse of fate in the simple future, seen through blackout darkness courtesy of Pacific Gas and Electric…

    One spread out like stubble at night. The fingers
stars, destiny the head explaining blank
records, numbered and erased accounts.
Swallowing one's tail, the tale swallowed one,
emitting either two or zero in that flash
of signal. Depends on how you count.

    How's that sound? Since you came to you came here
and since coming here you came each night into my bed,
leaving me curled in TV light across the room. You are
my shop steward. My environmental regulator.
My pilot light. My breathing apparatus. Mine, not
mine, solid and transparent. Between the lens
and the objective when the pupil opens up
to stare into the sun until inclusive
light refines that vision down to *nothing is.*

You might say *this is not life*. One answers
hey, you bright anomaly, anonymous
power surge, answer to my name. Answer
my name. Vocative other logic. Demon,
inspiring by discrepancy. The fly inhaled
with high-speed transport wind. Hey, say
something, something else, nothing else.

This is not life ... Life is splendid.

Let us therefore put a name to this dim profusion of shapes. Or rather, let us take away their names one by one, so as to admit that our fond memories of a shared childhood are all rooted in the dirt of a zoning tract that once housed a camp of tents and trailers at the outer edge, now incorporated and creeping toward a relocated center, of a city whose exemplary talent for concealing the violence with which its few areas of public density were policed had forced its homeless into the undeveloped scrub woods, and that here a shift in productivity came with heavy equipment, clubs, and stun guns to levy a newly-established bottom tier of differential rent — that bones were broken and shelters burned, these sudden movements and intense heats contributing energy to a physics of work that crusted value as new asphalt over the limestone and sandy soil, and that it is this amassing of cost from which we collect the sumptuous stuffs of our ability to recognize a common history in this place.

Your film treatment got at some of this, but I wonder, as I'd bet you do, about the obsessive worrying at the event-status of state violence whose vanishing beneath the threshold of your witness constitutes the perceptual field in which you have come to be conscious of your own struggle against it, whether it creates the resonating space in which frequency-spikes of allegory might break through the compression envelope, or whether it simply dissipates energy from that locale to create a dead spot, an impasse that can only give onto the cheap transcendence of an intuited "unknown world" that leads you astray by a show of mere coincidences, thus bringing us full circle back to the skin movie I was trying to seduce you with, before I realized I was seducing myself into position on the chair from which the question of an impossible perspective first arose. Would it matter if I told you, for instance, that I am writing this while eavesdropping on county planning officials who are busy congratulating each other for their political maturity in grasping that the true function of land use policy is to follow along behind "market forces," or would that only become, given the contained space in which we conduct our interrogation, one more illegitimate device for amplifying the private twitching in my throat into a wall of sound that would fill in the unseemly gaps in my command of the composition's unfolding?

 I am concocting alongside this a narrative of a woman whose body is always being replaced by its own skill at reading its angle of incidence with the reduced but fractally infinite scale of a suburban parking lot, a narrative that will run vertically through the blank horizontals of this letter, among the flowers that line its borders and bounce encrypted transmissions back and forth in a riot of duplication and surrogate objects, if you care to crane your neck for such a reading. This will bring you to mirror her posture and harmonize with her on a misplaced conviction in the generative force of minor retail while you pointedly ignore how much of the rest of the chorus rode in on Striker assault vehicles. As I work your letter *talks botany to me, but I scarcely listen. I am no longer sufficient in myself, I am now only the necessary intermediary between the heavy ordnance and you,* a sticky starburst through my abdomen that vomits light into the darkened passageway where you crouch on the far side of this clearing. Were I to ask you to send help you would take it as the worst kind of joke, one played neither on you nor on myself, but on the *situation* that binds us to the emergent form of our sitting here talking without moving our lips, an unwarranted grandiloquence that would redound to my own statuesque figure of renunciation while discounting the ropy strands of you that make my hair adhere weblike to the niche you occupy.

Of course, this caution about our dangerous day-dream has ended up counseling both of us to become more deeply distracted. In such a state I invariably discover that, *contrary to what I have always believed and asserted, I am extremely sensitive to the opinions of others.* Our names crack against each other like televised artillery. Nothing will restrain us from the ersatz ecstasy of that incomparable event, not even the misdirection of command that the control booth pipes in to the scenario you have so deftly placed between us.

Right back at you,
M.

Among the Flowers

        local color softens tops of walls
Backwards reconstruction in the concrete public trench —
              under this coverlid
    beelines down the block now literally smothered by —
The dead crowd the sides of the canal, and charge for water.
          …precisely, liquid in reverse
    falls to newer depths, someone's cellar opens
    up   limestone sponge   new world
    water depending lively on a   yes
        the year they burned the hotels down
        the right-of-way piles up as cotton waste
            from underneath, and round us,
some precepts, necessities of spending it to make it

Value   out of swinging scythe   *pictured—*
   walled in.
              ...condensing space in unconditioned absence
I mean   the fact that fabric *breathes*
   outset in philosophy. The floorplan
 is to level. Too level. Shoot air, rain debris
you call nickel   we call opportunity costs
that much   to put the hand back in, steadfast   fire
   chances a procedure, favorable weather, *whether*
         all in due time, or timing, Dogberry, will be
the broken indicator light. Sigh. Anticipate
       what comes of pressure
is that pleasure, particulate emissions   or
  what might have happened *down there*
54 million gallons phosphogypsum process water
in your care, this tiny patch of raw flesh
tough cladding

       my silence, complete
grace to stretch the neck for food
   two amazing arms, like the woman
            spoke the offer offstage
— like the choice example leaves the whole question of choice
   by which the substitute expanse replaces place.
         Make the leap   that   is horizon
    in its hood, its wires a priori
     body to reflect its evidence of sale —
   seen before, does not explain the letter of
that smirk. Unfed, livestock chew the roots. The petals blur.

Tenants' Union

Tender as automatic weapons fire a burst of laughter loops a long time in the framed space between any two trees. Follows a bird through smoke. We are all still awake. All still, all awake. The political officer holds a banner. Her hands guide our eyes along its line of flight. There is not one bird but many. Our hands are nests that work holes into the smoke with every shot.

Is this what makes a home? Let's see. A zone without title is either like a market square in an old city, or a hole in the city taken to market by the square foot.

"The night is like a sack of merchandise," she instructs, "in which we are soon to be delivered. Where is the little scholar now? Who will tell us that our revolt shall never have existed? Motherfucker lost weeks tracking our fierce good humor, in and among these trees. Meanwhile only one of our sunsets has flamed out. Our time of intensity is a rapid flicker. It hides us from him inside strobe-frozen flashes. These he misunderstands as death."

I should have died in and with that sensation, I should have let myself be slaughtered without offering any resistance, without a movement, a bee drugged with tobacco smoke that had ceased to take any thought for preserving the accumulation of its labors and the hopes of its hive, weighted down as I was with a language made to bear the vertical impress of all the clandestine cargo of the clipped, repetitious phrasing in which the collective aspirations of the guerrilla band had stowed themselves.

"Hey! No talking to yourself. Do you have a thousand bucks to trick us all out with decoder rings? No? Hey, I can hear you, dead man!"

A heavy hand to the back of my neck, as punctuation. Like oil saturating sand. I fall into a joyful stupor in which urban architecture no longer displaces politics with elegy. We are all still awake. The next time you see us we will be so, still. We will be so still, organizing all the dead on your TV.

Field Recording

<Mission Day 2, 06:17:49>

After closing time the parking lot of the mini-mall filled with lifelike adolescent analogues. Their patterns of social intercourse are organized down to a remarkable degree of detail, and one could almost take them as real, live boys, so to speak. I'm sure you've had the same briefing with the exomusicology team that I received, though, and are aware that the proximity of the boys' houses to the Place has subjected them for a dangerously long time to the Warbler Madrigal Replacement procedure, and that they are, for our purposes, almost certainly dead. Knowing what that might mean in terms of their potential for counterintelligence, I still decided to remain in the field to observe discreetly, until an unfortunate incident forced me to change my mind.

I was standing in the middle of the parking lot transmitting my report of yesterday evening (can you get Engineering to develop a transmitter that works better from covered positions?), when a group of the analogues approached. I think they were drawn by my posture, which was probably outside the tolerance range of their mall-behavior simulation matrix, given that I was staring directly into the setting sun and subvocalizing convulsively, trying to wrap up the end of the report. (Another note: the Integral Communication Rig requires a great deal more skill for subtle operation in the field than it did in training situations, and this could become a liability. Talking to yourself in a crowd, even a non-human crowd, will *always* draw attention — and not often the kind you want!). Anyway, the group approached to a fairly close position, then stopped as their apparent leader, a "boy" of sixteen or seventeen, marvelously simulated in all particulars including downy mustache and permed mullet, stepped forward pointing and laughing.

The laughter was terrible. Yes, it was frightening, but what I mean is that it was badly done — kind of a shrill whine that sounded for all the world like twenty or thirty guitar amps feeding back in tandem. I mention this because it might be useful at some later date to know that the Warblers haven't gotten a handle on all of our behaviors just yet. If their infiltration breaks the quarantine, this information could in fact become crucial. Anyhow, overwhelmed by the extreme sensitivity to auditory input one experiences when in transmission mode (another liability of the ICR), I let rip with an involuntary peal of the same throat-shredding laughter. The two of us stood there for some time, ten minutes or so, squalling at each other like that.

What I'm leading up to with this is an explanation for the delay in filing my second report. Having participated unwittingly in a behavior mode that the Warblers' analogues seemed to understand much better than I did (at least that was my suspicion), and not wanting to explain myself to every inhabitant of the Place, human or otherwise, who might question me on some particular of this ritual that I'd missed or misperformed, I retreated to a dumpster located behind the installation, where I have set up a secure base of operations. This keeps me out of sight after sunset, which, if last night's example holds, is far more a crowd scene than "business hours" here. I trust you will see the necessity of this decision, and my consequent inability to transmit until after sunrise, when I was able to re-emerge onto open ground. Still, sleeping alone in a metal bin with that laughter still looping around me hardly feels like a model of operational security.

Adding to this unease was the state of disorientation in which I found myself when I rose from my bed of sour-smelling milk cartons and piled hair clippings this morning. For nearly an hour I was unable to focus my eyes, unable even to distinguish figure from ground in anything around me. What was worse, this problem seemed to overlap several sensory registers, up to and including my own proprioceptive orientation, leaving me stranded in place, unable to negotiate an object-world in which everything seemed to be simply a modal expression of the same substance. Trees and dumpsters kept absorbing and mutually liquefying each other, while my hands crawled up my own back. Even closing my eyes and navigating by blind touch was no help, as everything felt to my skin like only more skin. Finally, I realized that if I hummed a tune I could hear a small degree of difference between my own voice and atmospheric sound. Thus I was able to translate myself back to myself by echolocation, becoming like a grain of sand abrading the oily horizonlessness of the Place.

By now I hope I've succeeded in giving you the wholly accurate impression that nothing comes easily here, and that our training scenarios could never have anticipated the magnitude of distortions we'll have to operate within. Everything feels like a difficult, probably unnecessary struggle. So I shouldn't have been surprised that my separation from whatever it was that the Node had tried to claim me for by "smudging" me into the thick background of the Place became a new occasion for panic, as my fears quickly swung over from a threatened loss of self to an extreme paranoid defense of what I perceived as my hard-won boundaries. This in turn gave rise to invasion fantasies whose visceral reality I can still feel twinges of, taking the form for me of a certain knowledge that something was growing in my abdomen. I could see it, inwardly, a pink and veinous arborescence slowly pulsing its tendrils outward toward my limbs and head along the pathways of my circulatory and nervous systems. (For what it's worth, I remember a conversation with my mother in which she narrated for me a dream very much like this dating from the first trimester of her pregnancy with me). This alien interiority, I was sure, planned to use me as its means of egress into a larger world on which it had laid a colonizer's eye. It was wide awake and planting banners along lines of flight emanating from my body, chief among which, I fantasized at that moment, were these encoded transmissions demanded by our surveillance protocol. As if the Warblers — as near as anyone can tell a life form closer to the fungal than the animal — could somehow have developed the instrumental intelligence to decrypt our transmission algorithms, and were using the very language by which we hoped to effect their containment as a vector along which to propagate themselves beyond our *cordon sanitaire.*

What snapped me out of this unhealthy reverie was the sudden appearance (or maybe they just suddenly caught my eye — I'm sorry I can't be more precise) of two male figures, seeming remnants of last night's festivities. They were standing half-hidden behind an ornamental azalea hedge and talking animatedly but not, I couldn't help but feel, to each other. Rather, each mumbled separately to himself as in a trance, all the while hurriedly exchanging money and small plastic baggies in a series of calculations owing more to numerology than numeration. The effect of this scene on me was so startling that I only managed to forestall a moment of real panic by digging down into childhood memories and breaking into an old marching song that my grandmother had taught me as a little girl. For the sake of a comprehensive field report, I replay it here:

Won't study on no sickness
And I ain't go no call to die
Nor toil evermore, evermore

Wait, that's odd. I have before me now a very clear image of a bird. I did not know that it had built a nest in my hand, but now it has escaped through a hole in my palm. Also, among the flowers where those oracular boys appeared, a few identical blooms have traded places. The net effect of both these changes would seem to be zero, but I would advise further study. I insist on my perception that something has happened.

A more serious matter still, these mathematics of the morrow, the same as yesterday, in whose problems we shall find ourselves inexorably involved, govern us even during these hours, and we alone are unconscious of their rule, as of the vertical impress of interminable series of clandestine second languages upon our own, which we bear with us from place to place without ever speaking.

Did I just say that? Out loud?

Alright, the transmission log confirms that it was my subvocalizing that slipped that basso profondo sentence into the datastream. At this point I'm beginning to feel that I'm not much more than a sack for delivering the merchandise of this place — this Place — to you. You should know, though, that there's a lot you'll never get. So much of it adheres to my outside. For instance, right now I'm poking around for evidence in the hedge I mentioned. I'm not so sure, in doing so, that I'm really clearing spaces to peer between branches, so much as the branches themselves are drawing back slightly in order to make a mold of my body out of air. Memory regressions are flickering along my skin. It's like the light or some vibration here were calling them to the surface. My aunt is drowning in the bathtub somewhere behind my left knee. And my first boyfriend — I was sixteen, I think, a year before we moved away from here, which places him among the replacement dead who stuck around — and his close-cropped head, and my thighs squeezing, and him breathless, and his little tongue rough like a cat's, licking, and all this intense sensation is localized now at the crown of my head. There's a string of pure, exposed nerve stretched up from there, taut, holding me upright, being gently plucked like a car antenna in a breeze. I'm about to meet someone I've never seen before and I know that this will make me supremely happy.

Alright, there's nobody here. No image to paste down on top of anything, or frozen as if time could be a strobe light isolating posture from gesture. And this noise of nothing coming is like the impossible bodily injunction: "Be free."

I have to go now.

There's too little out here for me. For anyone. Include me out for a while and it might come into focus, or into tune.

There's a nonexistent revolt on the horizon to make sense of all this *singing*.

<Channel is open. Please close channel or reinitiate transmission. Channel is open. Channel is open…>

On-Mike During the Commercial Break

...or even grasp the distinction between the storyboard and the star.

Cut that wire, the one that ties
the ladder to the banner, banner
to eye-level pyramid displays.
Fall headlong into the aisle.

Judging from the *threshing* on the dormitory
floor, there was a trauma magazine to
read, or chamber that would store the grain of that
performance. No one wanted to be bothered.

A fifth advice column in the weekly trades:
"Send venture capital out ahead of witnesses.
The warden will officiate another supplement."

> And the doctor sticks a needle in
> a motor sounding down
> the block, down the black
> gulches of a city night rolling
> through an outage through
> power as a rout of feeling

for or feeling out the route those first few
tries. And then the scream. Of tires. In the dark. And
then the rush. Downstairs. Meet the crash survivor.
Censure her for peeping up through cracked floorboards.
So she lost another one that hated her, or one
she hated losing. Making sense of that one's more

than half the game. So they all failed, and everything
they'd struggled for paid twenty-five a week.

He'd save drops of it, from time to time, collected
in the white jagged ends of hospitals. The doctors
soon discovered two vertebrae ringing off
the hook and took another side, to wit: one had

one's life. One life. One owed
for last month anyway.

Openly, one agreed. Silently, that's one
more minute's overbilled long-distance.
And he wonders where that call had come from,
as she wonders whether one should make the call.

Term Paper on the Limits of Field Recording

Once you begin to decipher the language of misdirected command that slips a halting message into the unintended rhyme of the north county rancher's NRA billboard with the power ballad bleating from a passing car, or the subtle alignments of assonance that take a police raid on public housing in a car-crushing steel dinosaur on loan from the monster truck rally and brush it quickly over the constant murmur of drowned voices from the storm sewers, your harsh feedback squalls of laughter come at ever shortening intervals, finally merging into a continuous blanket you throw over your relation to the world, less a series of occasions than a process of metabolism that can only marvel at the chunks of social matter it passes undigested, your entry upon an indefinitely extensible American adolescence being already a kind of adulthood in that it is the outcome of the catastrophic loss of some particular gland that would have manufactured the one enzyme needed to complete the process, and as you walk through the city with the secret messages that are perhaps only the devalued byproducts of the impossibility of clear reception and the profusion of radio crosstalk on this cheap equipment bouncing around inside your head, you know that you have become not the promised body without organs that would have been congruent with your times, but a body with a surgical scar, living out its days on a special, restricted diet...

CROSSTALK:
...*an organism built for scrutiny, not speed.*

>   This one-sided side of the bargain. Ruled default
>   gets you people ready, case-hardened to intend
>   the train that comes to what's, in any case,
>   any case at all. At just about that legislated
>   time, minus time off for each doubt of any
>   meaningfully tracked and tied behavior, there
>   are members and membranes shielded with background,
>   greasy denim of the job at hand shunted
>   onto sidings, and in landscaped parallel
>   the lading list of gendered figures laden with
>   vulnerabilities of example. Service, side out.
>
>   A highest court ruled yesterday, inducing grounds
>   for that which shall have come to threaten one today
>   with college, knowledge-work gathered up in its facility:

disciplinary action, instant foodstuffs, technique
and technicality of promise deferred through each
                    and every lasting instance.

                    Juvenile desperadoes
                    inspect the armed robot.

        This one name, an invitation.
        Our stupid masquerade where,
        in general, one gets anonymously
        spanked. But in particulars
        "in person" one presents the rump
        of habit's kind stand-in for the ally
        once considered in the categorical
        question — namely, whether such
        embarrassments, worked over thus,
        grow flush with wage-equivalents.

And thus the sordid doings
through which one acts definitively
wooden, boy or girl boring
gimlet-holes of boring
trepanation into blocks
engridded on the blocky
frontage of a headspace.
Take a vista full of property
and character. Stick it in my face.

              Sores of activity,
              realms of exemption.
              Stick figures hurt

              for real by the fiction
              of the geometric point.

The official survey
measures off ground to
exculpate the audience's
ethical turn away from
stage business to the
qualified, finessed
mechanics of a plight,
a plaint. What's sung about
sings about the space, brings
noncompliant rafters of
the nonplussed house ringing
down, singing tinny in the ear.
                        The more it's true
                the more it's one more
                length to subsidize the course
                of studied affect: "I'm
                that very single, singing
                individual, who wears
                his heart upon his best
                behavior — that's a rule,
          a law, and a regard
          for all the earthed, unlettered
          spirits of the literal."

Call it natural ability. Years pleased to hear
the accidentals in the playback of
the piecework we'd recorded, years
to gestate infantile discrepancies
in timesheet after timesheet, developmental
narratives of epic scale to reach the very

outburst, the "of course" to round up posses,
dust off and authorize the use of force.

    This shootout here's for you.

    This answer of distant winds.
    This this and this, incontinent
    ideas in a motion blur,

    some partial recall of the partials all
    along the deadman's instrumental curve.

    Having tired of the discordant rush of overlapping codes in the malls and skateboard-scarred bank plazas, I had taken up for some time an ethnographer's position in the cavernous school cafeteria, following Birdy's map of esoteric knowledges into a scene in which it was a simpler matter for me to cross my eyes, let my jaw go slack, and mumble happily to myself while the miscellany of others blurred, converging on a compact mass that I approached again and again with the hope, always frustrated, that it would become a field against which that much-desired third voice the pursuit of which had never graced me with anything more than a stream of snide fragments, might finally sing a robust and fully-formed aria, this hope becoming over a time a bitter irritant as the hazy field against which I strained to trace its sharp contours brought into focus always and only the unlimited substitutability of the objects of my desire, as my attention rested with equal lightness on a girl named Dolores, a boy named Vatic Bill, a series of siblings lettered like specimens, and somewhere just out of the picture, but coloring it like reflected light, an aunt drowned in her bath, parents conceived as placeholders for positions I could not allow myself to occupy, a grandmother who would point out a clear path into a future not swamped by this clogged sump of present time, all of them participating, it seemed, in a collective life which, although false, was at least substantial, while my particularity of vantage, with its view toward edges of things emerging from their midst, held no more of truth and rewarded my scholarly persistence with nothing but a dry-throated cackle sifting over interminable one-liners. *When, even without knowing it, I thought of them, they, more unconsciously still, were for me the mountainous blue undulations of the sea, the outline of a procession against the sea,* translating for me the oracular pronouncements of the sea, always the same and always sounding as if overheard, or a sentence in a fraternally chiding letter meant for someone who, though resembling me, was a different person with different issues altogether: "Fundamentally, your highest ambition is simply to be well-liked." I had never before thought of the sea as such a political animal, but there it was, the fundamental law of the low, diffuse, palmetto-dotted city itself, a law whose highest civic good was to efface the marks of ministerial presences with their mysterious bags of severed heads, neighborhood uprisings repressed, reserve armies huddling under tarps in the unlicensed zones, the dead only remembered when some drain or other backed up, a law whose only exemption was to be found in the sea that so visibly linked this matte sprawl of sunburn to an exterior in the sphere of empire, but now it was the sea itself inscribing the text of the law in the bright glints that prismed from its oily swells, as if it were now possible to follow across its surface our many occupations that more and more resembled occupation plain and simple, all the while blithely dismissive of the pipelines, refineries, and associated artillery that bristled along its circumference.

Slowly these speculations flowed together with a rising clamor from the neighborhood outside the school, itself oceanic in its depth, though it crested at a sharper pitch, as a raid on a nearby unlicensed zone and "an incident apparently involving the burning death of a man who might have been a suspect in a serious crime" — to take it verbatim from the breathless local newscast on the transistor radio I still held by reflex against my ear — pushed hundreds of the previously invisible into the streets in a pitched, one-sided battle with a heavily armed police battalion who hurriedly converted the cafeteria into a command post, the school principal meanwhile hauling out of the supply closet where he slept the sweaty, pink-cheeked former professional wrestler kept on hand by the district as both entertainment and object lesson — such being the times, I tell you — for an impromptu pep talk in which we were instructed that the appearance of disproportionate lethal force arrayed against the ragged crowd now pinned down in an intersection was simply a contrast-effect of the light, the sun being especially bright that day, and that it was supremely important to avoid "jumping the gun" — his words, without irony — and ascribing any definite political content to the massacre, lest in our haste to do justice to the dead and wounded we turn the whole battle into "the worst sort of joke — a joke on our very *situation* itself." Whatever value these events might hold for agitation would be crusted over with new asphalt by the day's final bell, though *if you looked more closely at what you took for speed bumps you would have been able to give names to the figures curled beneath them.* This was the hurried counsel whispered by my former beloved Dolores, always held in high esteem by her family and mine for her ability to fold twice the language into half the space, as she raced past pursued by a detachment of the riot squad, not even breaking stride as she tossed a concluding word at me over her shoulder only to have it crash against the muscular grunts of inspiration from the beefy exemplar at the podium, the two urgent exhortations canceling each other in the air and forming a hollow in which I heard, in negatives of filtered speech, "Once you talked to the trees and hardly heard a word, but now, having grown smaller, you are prepared to receive an account of what twists among their roots."

    Relief washed over me as the long-awaited happened all around, the atmosphere itself to which all experience had been reduced breaking open on the sure knowledge that a spike of something green and new was ready to burst through a hard soil compressed almost into stone beneath the onslaught of machine treads and ground rent. *It was the most intimate part of myself; and so I had never been able to look at it with detachment, to extract emotion from it, until this day on which I encountered it, realized outside myself, in the body of a girl* who tossed it aside as an impediment to her becoming, someday, a woman standing in the heat of a parking lot, speaking to me in a new language while she gauged the angle of incidence between herself and a minimal landscape in an effort not to vanish altogether. I knew then that I could do nothing to shield those assembled in the cafeteria from an explosion that was sure to come, and that I must return to the woods, no matter how many times I had repeated this decision, no matter the weight of all the volumes of independent studies the man from the Redevelopment Commission lobbed through every window between here and there, if I hoped to find the woman who had raced ahead of me in time to live in the private twitches and unseemly gaps of a world of analogy on their far side.

Oil and Water

I had been wandering for some time, map in hand, over leveled and sifted ground whose soil, a fine gray powder that caked the topographical lines of my body but stayed placid and still upon the earth itself, was uncompromising in its revelation that nothing stood to cast a shadow, and that nothing further would ever again grow to such stature in such a place, everything one could call position vanishing into air as a gentle proxy for the legitimate means of violence, when a sudden effect of "rounding up" or "rounding down," whether the land bulging into convexity or the blank blue sky swelling in anticipation toward a place where something would have come to stand revealed had I arrived a moment or two sooner I could not tell, jammed the two planes of my experience together hard and brought me face to face with what occupied the newly vacant, ashy zoning tract. Row upon row of swivel-bar lawn sprinklers drew curtains of water back and forth across the land in a series that seemed to extend its converging lines well beyond the limits I intuited for the newly zoned plot, or rather they built an ephemeral architecture, the primordial arch repeated as a decorative element that swayed and quavered in the slight breeze and in fact collapsed at its apex into a drift like fabric, each point along the curve where this undulation met the ground blooming in a puff of ash that swirled for a moment or two in the intervals between strands of falling water, and between the drops that composed each strand like a string of ornamental beads, the complex interactions of particle matter rendered liquid in the air and liquid particularized in luminous drops giving rise to the shapes of an alternate ending, in which the previously visible carried a wave of temporary habitation across enclosed acres, not uprooted because not striking down to bedrock and thus not subject to the kind of displacement by which I might have entered the scene as one of nostalgia, but lingering as if the remnants of fire and exhausted soil might constantly shift from the ground to bear the impress of a face I had never seen before except whenever I looked into water cooling and going sour in the bathtub and remembered that it was the haste of my reaching after conclusion in the form of a place from which to begin that had structured the cruelty of afterthought in which my dear Auntie Terrible had met her end, exposed now for the first time in the medium which overwrote my own face in shades of gray that smeared it gradually into the parcelized real estate, so that the dead woman who would not leave and I who would not be permitted to remain as a figure against that miniaturized horizon might meet on some middle ground where every gesture vanished into the further potential and propensity for convolution and lush rituals of hide-and-seek, as indeed the powder underfoot could be counted on to shift but not to bear a footprint for longer than it took to take the following step.

"*Fallen now, situated outside her own type in which she sat unassail-*

ably enthroned, she is now just an ordinary woman, in the legend of whose superiority we have lost all faith."

I think the voice was mine, but even now I would not swear to it, coming upon me as it did like a solid block of matter which the intuited presence of a social scope for my movements across the inverted pastoral of suburban zoning had lifted as if on the shoulders of a crowd composed solely of iterations of the person whose death I had not yet finished writing, holding it above me where the television signals bounced around the high-tension lines and scaffolded metal towers, until the assembled mass simply grew tired of waiting for me to look up and let it drop on the top of my head, forcing out a sentence like the squeak of a favorite childhood toy suddenly noticed in the hands of the kid across the street, who pounded it mercilessly, delighting in the tortured expression of wheezing air from within that had, until then, provided one with a unitary and private text of origins.

TELEVISION [signal bouncing wildly off Heviside layer]:
Is there something stuck to me right here?

> The need accorded to bizarre collections
> of formaldehyded heads. The formalist's
> description of death. A place of air
> and track lighting, drowned in radiance,
> all visible distinction rearranged
> ingeniously as mirrored fragments,
> jigsaw fashion.
> > The deckhands partied on
> > the several shores again.
> > Guitar and *tres*
> > strummed soft across the hard

    narration's edge of a bloodied
      sea as allegory
      of the sawtooth wave that always
      seemed to rip the outer
      partials raw with amplitudes
      of inflammation. Tear them
      loose from fading to the tonic.

    One remembers staring blankly
    at a moony round of face.
    Remembers even when it fills
    the present frame, an opening
    folded very fast. Like superlatives
    of definition, description,
    ice, alcove, surface of machined
    and burnished steel, perfect matte
    to finish saturation with
    a self-effacing almost sheen.

Maybe I'm delusional.
Maybe you're a pattern, or
an implant rooting into
…me, it, them, whatever —

  a scaly embryo to
  scale with another size
  entirely, pronominal
  by cannibalizing names.

And then the usual sad story: the monster, insectile but with human mucus membranes and a close kinship with our own imaginary genital malfunctions, dripping snot and cautionary biomechanics, vanishes into yet more New Age forms, stylized classicism, and the road-salt contours traced on mudflaps that do little to keep the sticky films away from your forward view as they pass, confidently untouched by radar. Despite the well-placed grit, some things remain intolerable for their polish. So robot-mindedness and laboratory clinicism get preemptively stranded, relocated in the late eighties, its precision and track titles — *Clear the Wired Megalopolis,* or *Emergency Third Rail Power Trip*. After that record hit the clubs we all became other than our previous selves. Uncompensated labors were our pseudonym producers. The outdated rhythm programming still works inimitable changes in our iterated gestures of today —

        lights, the scene / a too crude accent

Let's see that tongue you're sucking down
Loud, assertive, awfully dear

        slab length supernumerary meat

    Simply standing where I stood became intent, act, and guilty retrospect enough for an unlimited series of value-added transactions in deed and title, and the city rushed toward me across the erasure of monuments in the burned former forest, the rush being the form of that blank ground itself, a chain letter in which it would be discovered that, misaddressed as it was, and applied to an enclosed reality having no commerce with my own, I was nonetheless signatory to the author list at several points along its serpentine elaboration. In other words, the labor of dying my retrospective walk advanced through the clearing of occupation as a simple assumption in a single tense could be no longer silhouetted against a horizon of disappearance, but cut high-contrast photographic runnels down my face as the sprinkler system staged its clash of civilizations with the dirt that had by now thickened my features, gouging out from my forehead and cheeks a stage on which would play the drama that would finally allow the displaced violence of foundation, of which we might despair but ultimately wash ourselves clean, to percolate and sift through the fresh elemental admixture of wet and dry that piled up the deep nap of every tactile nuance in which one experienced one's angle of incidence relative to any site whatever, *every plat being a fresh universe in which, coming under the sway of a new moral perspective, we fasten our attention, as if they were to matter to us for all time, on people, forced migrations, markets, all of which we shall have forgotten by the morning.*

However little to be commended, there was a degree of refinement in this far beyond my youth of riotous acne and matted, sticky hair, as though I had come already to understand that on this site three-bedroom units would cluster around a golf course in whose every softened contour of irrigated grass I would read indelibly as I rode the lawn tractor for minimum wage plus the occasional free beer in the crew cooler, the present history of a landscape inexorably riven between the assaultive economies of oil and water. Thus it was with the pose, if not yet the conviction, of indifferent sexual assessment, that I greeted the arrival in the dead center of my field of vision, as he stepped out from the shade of one of the absent and uprooted pine trees whose colonnade I still assigned by rote or after-image to the measured lengths between the sprinklers, of a wolfish boy, older than me by enough to sport a slight growth along his upper lip and sharing in the grubby uniform and overstimulated facial muscles of the gang of boys on hand-me-down bikes who had set up around so many of my evenings along the margin of a plot of woods, about which I could no longer retain even the certainty that it once occupied the place I now stood, such a disorienting eddy of speed-bright commotion, the pinpoint pupils and hot flush of which marked him as well, who introduced himself as Bottom Dog with a sneer that scattered threats on the ground before him to carpet my invited entrance into the track of shuffled retreat his face seemed to recede along into a room full of objects and instruments just the slightest bit too small for him, so that one imagined him always having his knees jammed into his chest, or his arms pinned at the knobby elbows against his waist, his whole luminous flesh of erotic mastery and failure culminating in the obvious strain with which he barked at me, "There's a girl over there with a fuckin' mouth on her, and she wants to use it on you."

Since "over there" covered a distance whose measure was not length or even time but impacted masses of lost detail, every subdivision of any one of the infinity of possible paths, all tending toward it across a perfect dry flatness lit by a sun that gave out light only in volatile sparks, like a dusting of glass from some unseen window explosively decompressed, tending to proliferate and foliate into immensely complicated canopies of impossibly multiplex monochrome, there was quite some way to go, and having nothing to look at on the way, we saw literally everything, as in one of those insomniac nights in which the revelers down the street keep one blanketed in an itchy insomnia that throbs towards breath from where it lies prone and paralyzed in three inches of water, unable to lurch up and gasp in the certain knowledge that the air is a chemical agency that will bring the contradicted flesh exactly the knowledge it desires and avoids at a cellular level beneath the scrim of pronouns, unable to lean one's head out the window and quiet the party, or stumble into the night to join it, knowing that one's presence will be the final bit of heat over a certain threshold that will flare the sniffing sensor-pits on circling helicopters whose terrible vigilance never wanders too far from such scenes. And so we bored into the texture of landscape architecture's minimum there in the mixed-use barrens, as it bulged and rippled from the sheer lush excess of its own orthogonal strictures, until the opacity of what we walked into yielded pores, honeycombing the surface of sight with facets and filigree in the unalterable service of our successive personalities faithful to this charcoal sketch of a city sloughing off layer after unbearably bright layer, through which, like the brightness from an eye whose lapse out of memory mocks and catechizes more surely than the voice it once floated atop in light vitality, a painted ball atop a jet of water, we saw the luminescent night gases rising from the bay.

Foundry

Something finished burning while I slept. Finished with sleep, I worked it up into a series of notes. The film treatment is dedicated to comrades who carried on the struggle into smoke. They vanish there so thoroughly I wonder whether I have seen them. Here I work up a wrapping, folding their negative space in paper to mutely repeat what must have failed to happen for me, in happening to them. *They become then, and for that reason, albeit idle, as alert as working-days, pointed, magnetized, raised slightly to meet an approaching moment.* It contains too little to establish any better focus.

This was all along about production. Staging a big, excluded Something composed of polyps. A central mass remains obscure.

Transmitted code signals me forward along a dead frequency:

> No clause is good so
> far along havoc, yet muttered
> and/or mended, I did need what
> matter arms to bend alloy
>
> into shape. Quilt, conflict: product
> often eaten, center wall of
> extruded slapstick. Instability manufactured
> apt global scale—maybe many selves

revise the uniform as rifts button themselves
clad. Sew, connect, cathect—and so
thin!—meanwhile, so shelled, solid
line discords, in every *there*

far eyes know. Glass, but in itself
an arrow, tends rows the profit shaves.

The smoke parts on my indifference to witness those who even now must be gleaning fragments of value and snack food in the swirling darkness to either side of my line of march. To enter the silent city from this direction is to clear a view for production of the molten present. Vast hoppers and buckets depend upon nothing. Depend from the floor above. It depends. There is a secret abode there to which metal returns by flowing backwards up the towers. Smoke behaves like water in this air. Meanwhile a utopian guerrilla army keeps out of sight and silent. My rewired skin falls away in patches that shine with light reflected from their undisclosed location. The transmission has raised a welt. Form of a question. What is the point of a film that sees nothing? What is seen in a view that is all scenario and no witness?

In the interval of these questions I have discarded the notebook unfinished, just inside the margin of scrub woods. Whoever wants to take it up is free to do so. I have taken up a new series of edits. They are not in my shot list, but respond to a script doctor brought in from outside. They force me to behave like smoke. They are free to do so.

I have become the equals sign in an equation being balanced elsewhere. Superheated metals weigh against inversions of gravity. So the face of the local enforcer signals to me at an odd angle, not through flames but through smoke. The face of flesh across the glass face of a bank tower. A screen. The city, evacuated of resistance. Reflections are free. Reflections are free to travel around corners here. *By retracing my memories I can, under cover of that identity and as if through an internal passageway, run through all these images in turn without losing my grasp of one and the same person.* Half of the uniform I wear on this mission is hers. This is my role. These unfolding events. Enfold my body in the independent will of a sibling. A masterpiece has been written on my limbs in the medium of another's discards and hand-me-downs. This equals: I was yawning and stretching out of sleep.

My body began to lose its heaviness, for I filled it with an idea, the idea that it was an immaterial creature. Then an incapacity for impact. Then the failure to have modified the shape of a script doctor to whom I had entrusted the care of a sequence of events. The sequence occupies a hollow city with an absent insurgency. I, an ambivalent fifth column adding up to one. My idea has returned. It weighs gravely in favor of my culpability, so I am free to scale in reverse down this architectural column. It had led me toward reflections. Triangulating, toward a vantage that would reveal the bodies that cast them.

This place is like nothing I have seen. Here images are disappearing in a stream of dead data. Toxic matter. My erstwhile comrades sing acidly a few blocks off. The city knows the words, every atom of it reverberating. A low shore shakes under hurricane surf.

Strip Mall Blues

<Mission Day 2, 11:38:15>

…and flushed, I can feel it, even if the monitors don't register any change in core temperature. And something warm is trailing off my lip onto the sticky asphalt, like dead data streaming along some previously disused conduit.

Alright, transmitting now: *How many observations, patient but not at all serene, must one accumulate of the movements, to all appearance irregular, of those unknown worlds before being able to be sure that one has not allowed oneself to be led astray by mere coincidence, that one's forecasts will not be proved wrong, before deducing the incontrovertible laws?* Section Chief Apex, why will you not respond? Why does the terrain itself project at me an image of you struggling forward into smoke that will not clear? Why will your clear transmission not come to wrap in some comforting repetition this negative space that I am becoming?

Repetition is the sparkling liquid at the edge of every mass here, and my limbs trail long cilia that are stroked into song by the shifting light. By this token I will reassure myself that *you are here,* a message hiding in plain view and spawning a variant infinity of reflections that crowd out exactly the vantage from which I might observe their originating body. My original body, I think I can remember that…. Now I am infinitely replaced, analogous. I think I understand — no, I hear, but hear it resonating in my lungs and sinuses and skeletal muscles and intestines — how the Warblers' piggybacking protocol works on us by working as us. The more I transmit from here the more you receive. And the more you receive, the more of the seemingly disorganized, turbulent wavelets that surf the crests of that carrier signal come through to you, licking at the surfaces of the hollow column of echoes that broadcasts your own signal. So, in turn, the more you ping me with queries and instruction the less I hear you, the more I am replaced, and the more my replacements hear of everything else. In this way I fear that the vigilance of every working day on this mission is raised by a magnetic attraction toward an emergent form that builds within it. It's as if something inside our speaking to each other is asleep and dreaming furiously, and this form that we dream without its ever occurring within us will take on a greater solidity than the particulars of rusting dumpster, beauty college, azalea hedges, asphalt, sweat and ropy strands of drool out of which my intelligence, aimed at containing its spread, is assembled.

There was one chance, I think, when I first arrived here, to cultivate the deliberate ignorance that would match an honesty of purpose in which the Place and its beautiful boys, half clothed in the obscuring greenery and cascading car-stereo guitars, might have stood forth as incomparable events rather than analogues for the sore spots in a memory of what was let slip the first time around. But this would have precluded the very nature of the mission itself as one of infiltration. Section Chief Apex, I am addressing you here, since I assume, given the turn things have taken, that you have assumed personal command over the control booth. I feel bound to remind you that fully half the uniform that announces me as enfolded in such a command belongs to you.

If a little day-dreaming is dangerous, the cure for it is not to dream less but to dream more, to dream all the time, until the central mass that accrues to all this production comes clear as an object with its own shape, weight, and situation. We are well beyond that option now. Soon the others will follow us.

There is a sticky, candy-colored star inside my abdomen. When I sing or vomit in the heat these are the rays by which everything in the Place illuminates everything else, an internal passageway fully the size of me as it is the size of my context. Through this passageway pass all the images freighted with steganography and melody, emerging without resistance into the bright sunshine and acrid heat that is their own effusion. The equivocal aspect of this, considered against a background of the uniform I still wear and whose purpose in squaring my limbs and amplifying the private twitching of my throat has not yet eluded me, sets up a charged field in which objects shimmer with unanticipated difference tones. This is nothing if not an irreducibly aesthetic element, one which rewrites my every moral and political intent — saving "the world as we know it," some kind of police action — as a song that was until now always aimed obliquely just past me from some unspecified elsewhere. The fragments of value I once stooped to glean from where they fell now stand to witness me as I awaken all the dead frequencies.

These words come to me from a discarded notebook I found, near the margin of flowers where the two boys held their strange conference, at the edge of the scrub woods behind the beauty college. Together we are configuring each other, the words and I, as instruments to sing endlessly of *the repentant criminals whose remorse and regeneration once formed the object of my political portfolio. We will buy a house in a countryside where mists attenuate the light; we will spend long hours looking at boys garlanded with showy flowers; we will collect sumptuous stuffs.* My skin is a more sensitive instrument than all these monitors and transmitters. Taut and shiny, it reflects the sarcastic grin of two boys who crouch inside the dumpster where I have sheltered at night. They are analogues and do not need to eat, but for the sheer pleasure of it they snack on my dwindling rations while I stand here melting in the sun, transmitting balladry to an undisclosed location.

<End transmission. No further transmission scheduled>

The Front Row Gets Wet Despite the Tape Delay

Association shrivels a discernible view:
the military monument's backward vista,
features forward of continuous English

single instance of escape the lips

in far-off space and small
homogeneous time

applause metered rhyme opaque
manners other words

concussive concrete brush

breach to make presentable —
by which to make it pain.

Up into accumulating atmospheres, recursive
flight-path of the drunken butterfly whose feelers drop
and droop condensing weight and mounting pressure,

                                                      and after

                nothing. Supposition's evening
                paper folded flat into the bin

Second plunge past
mythological marbles
lost limb / lost wax
harmon mute indexed
amputation amped

hanging in midair
midstream mobile
traffic island veering
absentee signed out

the dust blows forward
and the draft blows back
a thrown up citizenry
body blows of rough impression

      disciplinary roundtop bench

wheel impressed flesh
chock and wedge
angle of a power pole
to glassed ground

———

The Singer's Alibi

Putting on the put-on
like a cheap, tight suit
flushed from cover stories
close to the confining vest,

>the vault bursts open. Spillage makes
>and masks a functional identity.
>OK, I'm ready now: to build your case,
>corroborating witness by default; to make off

>with the linchpin in a minor scheme of witless
>pillage; to face the figure never screaming
>but I sing, sweet monumental pigeon
>mounting to the temporary stage of sparkling

>imitation marble, not so hard but every bit
>as cold. Your wildly withheld applause claps me
>drunk into a habitable tank, flows of carbonated
>glycerine for warmth, bare perception of those

>99.9 degrees. Your lovely body only
>slightly more for heat than mine, your effervescence works
>a sluggish nerve at best. Too much of *us* spread out
>too thin too soon between drink minimum and lush encore.

So I yelled savagely for tune.
Small-time brutality demanded:
"Answer me." I have this two-ply
face that belts itself, a string of hits
and hitches. Things happened quickly then.

<u>transcription from the field notes:</u>
at such commotion made low bow as cover. followed exhaustive and masterful study. full catalog of assembled gestures entered room and did some sweeping. walked directly to said survey marker. what said walked directly over to me. over me. all over me. finally impression that would take. my level sense of pop architecture building foyer for the auction. tourist of an answer walking through. cashing out. gone before long. back late for more. news got out. word leaked through papers. one for the record. books

        unbound and bent blank placid face
        straighten up the call for help
        whipped round creaking caster chair
        the grasping ornamental knob

    burst forward.
    stopped short.
    peeped upstairs.

<u>I cast my ballot in reflection *to diminish and repeat:*</u>
The looking glass wasn't wired for a chaperone, and that looked like a resolution to those attempts at fostering telepathy in the rapid, sociable growth of his debt. Of course, there were the usual cheap and furtive kinks, bought at unusually high interest: a woman with the manner of a child, a manneristic man chewing up the exhausted scenery of belief in adolescences that never came. Something awful happened then, but I was pulling on the sequins and my eyes bugged out behind that brightness. Keep asking and I might remember my way out of this outfit. Was that it? No, it's *sequence*, and it dwarfs equations by the trivial increment of dead weight thrown out ahead:

Infinity equals the transaction —
delicate head for terrifying laughter
outside in the street at night

around-the-clock police
surveillance unidentified
strangers floating by

>   a pointy ocean
>   a pointless granted
>   century or two
>   the fundamental
>   implant sex

>   Mad to get it into you inside me.
>   Underwriting slips you loose of inshore
>   shallows like a riptide. Policies of
>   mutual insurance for interiors
>   of mirrored value sink, slip under
>   from abstraction into concrete shoes.

Flickering midnight throughways link
these crime scenes to a dodgy proposition —
dinner entertainment always cliffhung over
crevices, bridging serial force across
the periodic gaps in a display.

>   Claims adjust in wall text.
>   Dust piles up at auction.
>   We all buy the collection.
>   But only some collect.

An Unfinished Historical Task or Two

Dear M.,

It seems to me that, in all the staggered circularity of this displaced chain letter, a more basic and troubling circularity has been illegitimately overwritten which, were we to catch some peripheral glimpse of it, would raise a fundamental question for this scenario that one of us, surely, has written, as we would come up against the need to reckon with an event whose exclusion from our experience first set in motion the series of forced equivalences by which we have staked out this miniature horizon for each other, and this confrontation would articulate our alignment with, even as it staged our separation from, those hundreds of the previously visible whose static hissing opens the dead air between us to carrier waves. There are gaps in this world we build that substantialize our sense of time, so that the derealized features of a beloved aunt who died in a cruel afterthought cohere as a solid block like the hulk of a demolished television set whose vacuum, uncontained, becomes the exact shape of what must have happened to place us here precisely by subtracting itself from us in order to become a landscape across which we could imagine the drift of a merry band of saboteurs, terrorists and intellectuals through our scenario which aimed, not at recovering the catastrophic occupation and fire, but at tracing precisely the tempo of an experience that missed it so as to address us as those who "shall have come to be."

But even this precision fails to account for the production notes secreted by the scenario, not as its interior, as in the familiar trope of the film within a film, but as its necessary and missing anterior, a place prior to the tempo of non-occurrence where the problem of missing time resolves into a paradox of space through the essential technique of an absent social mass for being in more than one "once" per place, so that packets of life in excess of its body spread through our script and the scene of circular relation into which it calls us, making the question not the easy one of a founding absence, but the irrational numerical expression of our own reflections distributed among all the objects and territories we survey in the form of their non-reflective obverse, in which even the pain of a prior disappearance cannot stabilize around those whose dead labor or labor of dying our situation here assumed, for *there is now the possibility of meeting them again later on; they have ceased merely to be silhouetted against a horizon where we had been ready to suppose that we should never see them reappear.* So it's not so much a matter of the uncertain authorship of those repeating phrases running continually up against the limits of a plot of woods already zoned out, as it is one of our own uncertain authorship of the guided tour that plods through their aftermath, an extractive economy of intelligibility and transmission that graces each of us with the luminous flesh of erotic mastery when triangulated between the sibling prior to us in the chain of duplications and he or she who follows. This is *the persevering and unalterable service of our successive personalities; hidden away in the shadow of the devalued suburban margin, despised, downtrodden, untiringly faithful, toiling incessantly under a charcoal-scrawled banner whose sole command is that it escape notice, and with no thought for the variability of the self as its iterations are marked by the row-planted trees effacing marks of productive consumption from a parcel of land, to ensure that the self may never lack what is needed,* save that lack which is the law of the city itself, and is the zero-sum hydraulics of a general need in the corpse-clotted storm sewers.

A laugh like a clash of metal survives the political funeral we diffused throughout the district of one- and two-story cinderblock construction simply by refusing to stage it at all, and so it is not yet clear what volatile spark might ignite a "difficult personality" or "personal difficulty" in a concrete parking barrier, an oilstain, or a dusting of safety glass across an intersection.

Distinguishing features, you should know, are in the habit of sliding uncontrollably around our faces like a bloom of acne — o substitute violets! in such detailed credibility —, and even jump from person to person on occasion, flat land and flat paper equally receptive to erasure and inscription, to the point that, had one of us not had the foresight to crop his sticky, matted hair there would be no telling us apart. *For he was one of those people who can never be "doing nothing," although there was nothing, in fact, that he could ever be said to do,* as if simply standing where he stood were intent, act, and guilty retrospect enough, his bemused stasis being all it took to transfer the land into its reality as value. Remember the school tour of the mid-state plantation, how it explained in minute detail the domestic economies of timber harvest, stock raising, and corn cultivation, leaving out only the fact that all this production was carried out by slave labor, and how, having slunk away later into the woods, we were chased back across a muddy stream by a swarm of hornets who stung our scalps, the general noise of their buzzing and our shouting spreading the exact texture of the day's events across our empty horizons of futurity? What I mean, I think, is that no matter the critical eye with which we return to that day's instruction, we must at least suspect that the ideological distortion remains a more primary moment, linked as it was with an ensemble of panic, physical pain, and the free-floating sense that the surrounding adults were liars as often as not, so that not the revelation of the lie but the swelling of anticipation pointing to the place where it *would have come to be revealed* was molded into the flesh itself, and a series of broken gestures in the knives, guns and bombs of such displaced violences is what has mounded up the dirt to make a seat for our simple facing off against each other here in this clearing, a simplicity that must have cost a fortune.

Watch your back,
E.

Bare Fat and the Lyric Root Cellar
(edited for daytime television)

    Piston into time and infinite sex —
    people will smile perhaps to recollect
    what quality of litigant might mean
    as unit quantity of forced decision.
    The genre works order to explicate what doubt?

And your ass will follow. Follow me out to the closing balance of a pluralist logic of ironic inconclusion. Allow us to arm our mechanical collusion with forced rigidity, automatism, absent-mindedness and gradualism self-correcting into smaller and smaller oscillations:

    margins shrinking round magnetic north
    american freestyle trading rhymed fours
    across the trading floor, trading off
    constructed time against the makings of
    a character. Statistically deviant, we laugh
        most every time
        a close-examined frame
        gets thrown around the
        banter of a least
        of photographic focus.

    Come rest bad feeling in the realm of un-
    necessity. The management invests
    the lying layman in the priestly robes
    of portent, cannot be accountable
    for items lost on premises of such
    conversion, and would not be accounted
    in the catalog of incident that

spills wet across your critical regard.
Not, of course, to think *activity* involved
in what gets named by naming you as such…

… though incident provide onlookers warm caloric stint of self-deceiving surplus, fake synthesis affecting simulation of the feigned disguise of mental magic cloaking anxious overstatement in illusion's mock-inflationary furtherance…

…the patient believed her father was the body
politics had stocked with figures: boss or state reduced
> therapeutic figuration
> great historical need
> tiny thumbnail real
> mortal figurine grow
> dead dark under earth

The Complete Works for Broadcast

\<Mission Day 2, 18:23:05\>
Our love becomes immense, and we never dream how small a place in it the real occupies, as we race ahead through the world's gaps into the simple substance of time.

Now my skin is glowing. My new skin, without heat. It metabolizes the social matter of the Place to become a portrait of myself. I will slip it between the pages of what led up to my arrival here, like a surgical scar preceding the knife in a backstory that was always only holding a place for my body. I have chosen not to see it again. So the hum of light shimmering along its surface must become the whole of what whispers in your ear. I know now that there was never any Node. The strange signals emanated from what your sending me here would make of what had always been misremembered or missed of the extractive economies waiting to speak through this ground. You have sacrificed me to this intelligibility. The transmission will not be interrupted again.

Without benefit of any signaling apparatus I tell you this. I *warble*.

This is the same as realizing that the sticky asphalt is the ground, solely. I have tossed out the most intimate part of myself into the intuition of interplanetary space, so that it might invade this patch of already invaded land and reshape me in the odd angles that are evidence of a primal vanishing that is the condition of memory for political operatives such as we. You at HQ will of course have your regrets. You wring your hands over what you have forced me to become in order to make the encrypted signal of all this come clear. These qualms I will not assuage by any advice mined from the sub-basement of my situation. *Wisdom is negative and sterile,* as it should be. Don't hail me for yet another monstrous birth. Life is big, there are things you've forgotten, and the bind of this is infinite. Laugh into the transmitter like a clash of metal and get on with it.

Something is on its way, *coming to the same as makes no difference.* And there it goes, the last of the sun. The Place is filling with a series of sibling analogues, all my brothers and sisters like letters in an alphabet. Or like exchanging letters across a leveled expanse of land use policy and empire, spelling out the backstory. The Warblers are not human, this much we know. What I have to report to you now, the news, is that they are the human form of an arrival after the human event. What cleared the ground for them is what happened here before the choice to remember or forget could be posed as such. We are dancing here, spelling it: a plot of woods, bodies mostly dark crowded into tents, fire mostly bright, apparatus hauled in on trucks, the leveling and grading, the cinderblock and asphalt transferring the land into its reality as value. Someone thought to make, of all things, a movie here. Which is no more than any of us, having made it all. The city grows, a cash crop.

The broken gestures of the knives still lying across one another, the swollen convexity of stone in the light of machine treads and ground rent, into which the sun introduced a patch of yellow velvet. In the eyes that only yesterday were situated at an infinite distance (where we supposed that ours, wandering, unsteady, desperate, divergent, would never succeed in meeting them) the conscious gaze, the incommunicable thought which we were seeking have just been miraculously and quite simply replaced by our own image painted in them as in a smiling mirror. I think I'm trying to tell you that since my new mode of broadcast has opened all your restricted channels to the general noise of their echoes, your field instructions are missing me. Missing me they spread into that empty city. You are speaking to those who trail behind a line of march to overhear. You are the sound of an investment in fifty stories of reflective glass. I have this on authority from a beautiful boy who has returned to the parking lot from a clearing in the forest that was plowed under years ago.

That clearing was supposed to have prepared the ground for something. As a malt liquor bottle clinks against the beautiful boy's teeth I am thinking of what comes next. It is dark. The clearing, because I came too late to take it up as an event, has become the ground it prepared. More flat land, flat paper. Landing strips.

Thus my siblings, who arrived here because their warbling needs space above all in which to realize the promise that all contents are replaceable. Not long ago the azalea hedges ringing this unit emplacement of exchange and alien possession talked to me. I heard more than words. Now, vibrating along with the drive to expansion that has become the new fundamental, I am transmitting my account of the negative spaces that overwhelm their twisting branches. You are unprepared for this.

Now, as if in order that the rich decorative ensemble formed by the lovely train of replaced adolescents, at once black and orange, greasily luminous in the sodium night, might freely proliferate before the clearing in all the variety of its forms, my siblings, with their shapely limbs, their supple figures, but so different one from another, come into sight in a cluster that spreads out as it advances towards my boy and me, but closer to the blank advance of the clearing, in a parallel line. Here at the devalued suburban margin, they are inviting us to dance and sing. It is the undiscovered law of the city itself: all marks must be effaced.

<18:29:03. Unauthorized transmission received on secure band. Attempting to filter>

AMBIENCE AND GEOMETRY/
SEATED POSTURE

>A speculating danger slightly
>more or else more slight than cruel
>bade them fetch the governed cities home.

>>Burned their bodies just enough,
>>pursed full of underhanded payoff
>>and so swelling from within to match
>>the surface tourist tan accrued in that
>>>annealing's wake in which square blocks
>>>of elsewhere got their otherwise reduced.
>>If all that's left is overhearing on the bus,
>>the conversation burns a stare at you.

>>As though Pythagorean numerocracy were
>>both dispensation and dispensary, permission
>>for my "let me count the ways" and count
>>of surveyed ways in sum, my darling, hear
>>my hand, hard put to uses of its craft —
>>that delicate raddle through the turnstile,
>>tick by tick by stitch. In exceptionally similar
>>exchange, could not explain and still began
>>to flag each tomb as it occurred, inverted
>>data sump within the file. Ascending

            more humane, the separated apex
            of the rising pileup one rides.

    The fairest groaning
    labors out, starting
    something like an engine,
    flow of power through
    spare parts, scrap metal — you
    light-reflecting recess
    no eye's discovered yet.

So that was the proposal: a coffin-shaped cavity filled with dazzling lines of sight blithely overrunning lines of force. On the monitor you can make out minor darknesses in lungs, heart, viscera.

        Abrupted
        Finelined.
        Totaled.
        Cut.

    Skin happened swiftly. They'd begun.
    Entrance was restricted using coded disks.
    The body-soul transducer doesn't turn, but hums.
    No moving cogs in trauma's work. Produced internal
    volume of the lancing static hiss considered
    as interior design. Stasis rises from the army

        of collectibles in miniature, heads
        arrayed in diorama's tight expanse.

    You can be God, if not a traffic camera.
    Fastened into portrait-framed small vastness,
    each being in an envelope of solitude, you block
    the scene with room for in-the-flesh dissolves.

All around, the mystifying shadow
of your vaunted hoodlum adolescence
has remained intact. The buffer drains
off surplus, keeping certain corners dark.

But the cast-off gun in every scene
was planted by the ever-present cop.
And your literal translation of generic *noir*
shows just how far the casting couch would go
to shunt the ammo dump to other bodies,
absolve your out-to-lunch imaginings of *you*.

But we are spring-loaded, and we do
spring. Sometimes even into motion.

The water fountains in the hall of justice.
Tough, regular faces line the stifling hall.
Perhaps you take a dive, crack the ornaments
of glossy-finished woodwork, and the odds

pay off, a gamble taken.
A counteracted sacrifice.
Ill-concealed weakness
in the kiss, *the living self*

pressed up against its symmetry,
dressed for trial or event. The
plus-sized "it," the negligible hand.
But reflex isn't all the grammar

for the out-of-context shape its twitching spells.

<18:32:44. Filtering successful. Returning to field agent's broadcast.>

In the crosstalk and complexity of steps, one by one they fall silent and disappear. This is the ringing hollow of my transmission. How foolish to assume that the Warblers, being inhuman and spreading by replacement, would function like a virus. Those masked packets of life-in-excess, propagating in the medium of our cells, are only the nearest human image of the inhuman. The Warblers effect replacement not by living in excess of us but by dying in our midst. Removing themselves from the scene into ubiquity, they have mastered the essential technique, lack of knowledge of which has blinded us to the shape of our time: how to be in several places at once.

There are figures curled beneath the speed bumps that could have told us this from the beginning. And with that I shift pronouns. We are hundreds of the previously visible crowding emptiness into your streets. Do not mistake the hiss of dead air for closure. We are all transmission.

<Channel open. Shutdown protocol unsuccessful.>

When Bone Pops Clean Through

isolate shape an acid etched
from hot airs' sum the summons
to drill tune straight into heads

toward daft tops of soft heaps
up as rubble or bond rates
color schemes toward phrase's turn or head's
cant along paid bylines offsite

furious an informant is beaten then shelved
over voting for transnational frame
of tale if my frames owed persona
to kinship then a longing and

trauma's property's reach into reproduction
doubles up over market projection

Business Improvement District

    The problem with belief is not that it lays a false assertion over true facts. The sun will rise tomorrow, we say, being false. This is not belief, or not its problem. The problem with belief is fact. In fact, the sun has risen. And is false. Layer after unbearably bright layer. This is the opacity of light in the barrens of architecture.

    The city, being vacant, has rounded us up. A fine gray powder drifts in from the horizon. It pauses, opaque, over the forms of cars and buses. They have joined the evacuation. Vacant, the city is choked with them. Alone, we choke on the opacity of air. We are corralled in what we have taken over. Rounded down to speed bumps. *The people who refuse us the objects of our desire are always ready to offer us something else.* Charcoal extracted from the hinterland, for example. Digital photography. My face towers over me in glass. Explosive decompression seals again my bond with the reserve army. They have turned a corner, away from me. I review our fate through screens that work both ways, but not at once. If you're shot by a helicopter that circles on the far side of that image-boundary, you're just as dead. You're not alone.

    Glass like a string of beads scatters reflections in every direction. The reserve army I followed here is absent and is multiplied into a crowd around me. Glass is flowers, leaves. It scatters itself on asphalt. Scatters asphalt, scatters ground. The ground is multiple. Landscape fractures and shrinks into miniaturized horizons. The sky is not a dome but a single arch. It collapses into shards of decoration. Garments smash their way out from behind display windows. We are slapped against each other. Red is the color of wet flesh. Wet ground. It bears our footprints. It will not bear us up.

A face framed in oily locks commands the heights. *Always that second face which a person assumes when she is absent.* The political officer commands the whole echoing city to send letters to me. Initials only. Need to know. Objects and instruments are jammed into the chest, the arms, elbows, knees, waist. A grubby uniformity disorients the dead center of every field of vision. The obvious strain with which it barks at me, *"Pleasure in this respect is like photography.* Falling is a greater faith than the legend of my superiority, which you still try to write, wearing my hand-me-downs. Look up. Every torn scrap of fabric left to us in these vacant buildings is our banner. *The beloved object is merely a negative, which we develop later."*

"I alone am escaped."

I will say this of our trip downtown. Then it will no longer matter, being clear. Being fact. Riven between oil and water. Rigidly unavailable to itself as an image. Whatever the city is, is not here.

This is the new forest. A mass lifted on shoulders of dead signals and metal scaffolding. It requires that I speak about a few things. Events elsewhere. I squeak. Elsewhere pounds me so I wheeze and become desirable. This is the city: fresh universes on every plat. My hands tingle in the deep nap of tactile nuance as I sift through gutters. Bargain shopping. Leveling the hinterlands. A radical republic squats the voids in brushed concrete and iron armatures. It encloses a reality that rushes away. A blank check having no commerce with the money it sheds into my palm.

Redevelopment

We walked for what seemed forever, the converging lines of small-scale irrigation and the vanishing point of our hopes in the distant intuition of the miasmic sea remaining inexhaustible, until finally the tempo of value in the municipal relation to the aquifer conquered the tempo of space in our walking as the mid-day water rationing kicked in and the sprinklers went dry, and the uncloaking of infinite circuits of carefully installed desert in the midst of the growing suburb threatened to derail progress altogether, until Bottom Dog hit upon the expedient of spitting onto the ground ahead of us in alternation, so that first he and then I would arc a sticky glob some few feet into the future, toward which we would trudge until even with its landing point, the air meanwhile still minimally romantic with the thin dust and ash thrown up by the impact and rendering suitably sublime any reference to a larger scope for our endeavor than that immediate ambit of a step or two, whose terminus having been reached, the spitter would stand glaring intently forward while the other stretched out full length upon the earth as if in worship, slurping up his deeded unit of moisture and thus forestalling collapse through the next repetition of the cycle, which now gained a teleology against the illusion of infinity through which it had labored to this point, as we now gauged our linear movement by the approaching finite zero of dehydration, strategically counterbalancing this against the infinite zero of the vanishing point, which continued to glower at us from where it squatted just atop a horizon which neither approached nor receded but maintained about us an enclosure, proving once and for all that the denuded landscape was fully and expensively dressed.

"Like all them trees was just bad hair due for cutting," muttered Bottom Dog as I lapped his precious froth, by now mostly stale air and grit, from the small hollow it had made in the dirt, frozen in the realization that the landscape suspended our recognition of its actuality precisely in this function of leveling its forward edge so as to point at what would be simply more of itself. Looking up, the sun caught me full in the eyes, surrounding each lingering mote of dust in the air with an angelic halo of deferral, a pleasant regret at the absence of an interlocutor blossoming from even the irreal remnant objects in a zone that had achieved a fine-sanded ideality, *and as I passed from corolla to corolla along this chain of flowers, the pleasure of knowing a different one would send me back to the one to which I was indebted for it, with a gratitude mixed with as much desire as my new hope.* It was in this posture, sun smearing my face and the featureless expanse of dust together, squinting and, I thought, thoroughly beatified with the inward expansion of understanding onto which my streaming eyes fell back, that I first noticed a deepening shade on the periphery of the obliterating glare, tracking in toward the spot where I might have focused had my eyes' fatigued muscles still had the strength for such deliberation, until it filled my field of vision, not so much blocking out the scene whose extremes of light I had been vainly trying to parse into contour, as suffusing it, toning it down as if it were a barrage of high-pitched white noise between whose source and myself an absorbent wall of acoustic tiles had suddenly been interposed, so that the source of this eclipse remained, for all it restored the world to a range of experience acceptable to my strained nerves, indistinct and hazy, introducing itself in time to the slow dilation of my pupils as only "That Other One," billowing toward the distant vanishing point and its promised occupant, whose attainment Bottom Dog and I had begun to treat only as an enabling fiction, in an insane lure of self-presentation, saying as if it were the gentlest maxim of encouragement, "You know she's impossible."

As I pondered what this revelation might mean for the course of our migration across the plains of redevelopment, residual brightness continued to dazzle, in decorative shards that ate into the structure they purported to reveal, the picture I was beginning to reassemble of my location in the world, and for the second time in my life I was graced with a vision of dancers just behind the level blank of visibility, that perpetual assistant Americana leaping in erratic, quantum spasms through the lacework of discrete perceptions that had not yet cooled enough to form a whole, and she in turn revealing a certain insubstantiality, or more precisely a differential substance, through whose variegated densities one could make out the wilder career of that subcutaneous armature of figure that was the assistant once removed, Melisma, parceled out into discrete and bounded units that constituted place by shifting uncontrollably through space, until the whole prismatic allegory bled together once again in the cooling gray screen of That Other One. The soft voice resounded once again, and in a tone of unlimited resignation and self-effacement left hanging in the air between myself and my companion the absolute command to empty out our pockets on the ground, in doing which we discovered that our meager reserves of cash had undergone an exponential growth, so that the whole process took some time and left our hands chafed and sore from digging into pants that bulged tight against this entry with their unforeseen burden of great wealth, which spilled out copiously and retroactively naturalized the plane of blank progress that we had been approaching until then as a neutral barrier. *"Don't think this means they'll let me play with you, dirt-sucker"* creaked a ragged voice, making its inescapable appeal to realism from somewhere beyond the mist and the hard line of horizon it blurred.

An excited panting at my side drew my glance to Bottom Dog, who was scampering in tiny circles around the still-damp spot from which I had drunk the most recent in our series of refreshments, reciting as if it were a text he had learned with great effort and even greater pride, *"But it is not then for us a series of different events: its ceremonies remain external to an unchanging face, vacancy in excess preparing the way for a grand entrance obscured in this gray drift."*

In the ensuing silence a low hum from somewhere back along our endless track rose to a clamor and then to a deafening noise as helicopter blades chopped the air into powerful wave-fronts that shunted our nascent friendship into a premature resolution, and though I am by no means proud of its effect, I retain my narcissistic admiration for the brevity and lasting elegance of the dancer's movement with which I shrugged off Bottom Dog and left him there, stranded between the two roles in each of which he had managed for me only the barest sketch of a performance, allowing myself to fade forward into the washed out tones of what That Other One did to the myth of our progress, as an epochal destruction arrested him at the apex of a joyful leap. The soothing tones of gray defeat buoyed me up so that I floated forward of a tsunami that was enveloping the ground, congratulating me on the acuity of my ear as I noted the overtones that metal, applied with sufficient force, brought shrieking out of the disconnect signal which the manicured desert, just beneath the threshold of my perception, had been giving off all along.

Radio:

<Mission Day 2, 18:34:00>
...AND WHILE YOU BUSY YOURSELVES IN USELESS SPECULATION AS TO WHAT IT IS YOU'VE FOUND PULSING WITH AN ALIEN LIFE, HEAVY IN THE PALM OF YOUR HAND, YOU TAKE NO NOTICE OF THE MORE ESSENTIAL SENSE IN WHICH IT POSSESSES YOU, A DEMON SPITTING CODE THAT DISTRIBUTES YOUR NEW INVISIBILITY ACROSS EXOTIC COMPLICATIONS OF SURFACE. YOU HAVE GIVEN YOURSELF TO TRANSMISSION. EVERYTHING KNOWS WHERE YOU ARE.

<18:53:47>
WHAT YOU HEAR IS THE PLASHING OF A MARVELOUS FOUNTAIN DISCONNECTING YOUR SKIN FROM YOUR SOUL. YOU MISS THE POINT, WATCHING OUR FACES TURNING VIOLET IN THE MIRROR. WHO ARE YOU CONTACTING THERE? *IT IS MYSELF, AND I AM IT.* THOSE IN

WHOSE SOCIETY WE THINK TO TAKE PLEASURE EXIST FOR US ONLY ON A FLAT, ONE-DIMENSIONAL SURFACE. PERCEPTION IS RESTRICTED TO THESE LIMITS. A GREAT WEALTH OF SELF-VALORIZING BROADCAST TURNS THIS PLANE INTO A VOLUME. I AM YOUR ECHO.

<18:55:00. Switching to a secure band>

...ALL THE SUPERFLUITIES IN WHICH YOU HAVE CLOTHED YOURSELVES. THE OVERFLOW IS RATIONING, AND WATER WILL NOT REFLECT YOUR FACE. IT REFRACTS THE MISDIRECTIONS THAT OBTAIN BETWEEN YOUR BODY AND THOSE WHO HAVE DRAPED IT WITH THE GREEN, WOODED PATCHES OF CITY PARKS. THE GRANULAR TEXTURE OF THAT EXPERIENCE IS THE MEMBRANE FOR A FATAL CONVERSATION BETWEEN ARCHITECTURE AND ACOUSTICS. AN AMPHIBIOUS AFTERLIFE EXCEEDS COMMUNICATION. SWIM IN THE STREETS.

I could never have believed that I should now be dreaming of a sea which was no more than whitish vapor that had lost both consistency and color, the form of my citizenship crystallizing in the static. Tiny flames dance there, and dovetail neatly with something prehensile in the air whose form is ownership. I interrupt this program...

<18:55:49. Losing transmission. Attempts to identify possible second sender inconclusive. Switching to public band>

They were gathered close round me, and between their faces, which were not far apart, the air that separated them traced azure pathways such as might have been cut by a gardener wishing to create a little space so as to be able himself to move freely through a thicket of azaleas. THE MEMORY-FOUNDATION IS TRUCKED IN FROM THE HINTERLAND. YOU HAVE COMMANDED US. WE'LL PLAY TOGETHER IN FORMATION IN THE FOUNTAIN. THIS JOYLESS UNIVERSALITY IS BROUGHT TO YOU BY YOUR OWN INTERIOR, WHICH BRINGS IT FORWARD IN A FROTH OF LANDSCAPE FULL OF ECHO. THE WORLD IS CROWDED WITH YOUR SOLIPSISM.

<19:03:33. Isolating second voice in crosstalk. Filtering.>

...when, on the other hand, I was lying on the grass among these siblings, the plenitude of what I felt infinitely outweighed the paucity, the infrequency of our speech, and brimmed over from my immobility and silence in waves of happiness that rippled up to die at the feet of these young azaleas... a vague dazzlement that had spread from brain to eyes. REALITY IS THE DESTRUCTION OF SHADOWS. COME INTO THE OPEN. TRANSMIT, MY ANGELS.

<19:04:01. HQ transmitting on all bands.>

YOU MUST WRITE DOWN THESE NAMES. VACANCY. RICH ARCS. OIL AND WATER. UNDERSTAND. WE MUST WRITE THEM DOWN. THEY FALL AND LEAVE US DAMP. THEY FALL AND LEAVE US. WE LEAVE US. UNDERSTAND.

Leisure Infrastructure

I will mention only in passing the ranks of leathery, emaciated figures who reclined along my path in plastic lawn chairs, gazing up without hope into sunlight filtered through the same damp, glaucous mist that interposed itself between my view of them and the scene they constituted, for to approach them too closely, even in memory, would be to follow out a certain narcissism to its culmination, allowing that those characters only who manage to write their names into the grime that streaks our faces and limbs, as if we were some ill-used delivery truck, are worthy of our loving regard and efforts to understand, and thus to assign the blame for our inability to love well or to love enough to the vast underdeveloped tracts of landscape that could not marshal the absolute mineral standard of worth by which to proposition us with enough magnetic force to sway us from a singular track, along which perhaps we would not notice the single foot erupting from the ground beneath each seat of nylon mesh, in a reversal of the familiar shot from films about the undead, the replacement of the hand grasping back into daylight by the foot pistoning through the crust signaling perhaps that the trajectories of the dead are not aligned with a return to the world, reinvesting it with a surplus that our own attentions and affections could not manage, but with a descent, as if the soil were a thin scrim concealing the adit of a complicated honeycomb of mining tunnels, toward which these bodies thought to leverage themselves by pumping their legs backwards, up against the underside of the plane of land that holds us up, and that it was only an excess of effort applied toward the goal of a transit fundamentally away from us that broke through and left their soles kicking uselessly against the withered thighs and buttocks of those who sat upon the chairs, too thin and almost weightless to function as the immovable objects necessary for these inverted zombies to push off against and resume their burrowing. And so even in memory I turn away, certain that *every body is destroyed when we cease to see it; after which its next appearance is a new creation, different from that which immediately preceded it, if not from them all,* everything knowing exactly where everything else is being no guarantee that the whole ensemble is not at each moment simply spat up, radically original, by a demon that pulses to a rhythm not our own on the far side of the polarizing mist.

    This long and complicated turning brought me at last through the fog, which parted in foliate branches between which space established itself as the masonry of a new edifice of negative experience, and as I stepped through this hedge-work I found myself again side by side with Bottom Dog, whose leap out of time had brought him here ahead of me to whisper in my ear certain confidences which I will not repeat, except to note that it was this encouragement that prepared me to approach the person now revealed in the replete blanks of arborescent mist, standing as if rooted to the freshly laid and still-sticky asphalt whose line against the plot of gray ash articulated a border more immediately felt, because more concentrated and absolute, more audacious in its gesture of inscribing a line around the infinite, than any territorial definition of nation, and who, no matter how many times I circled her, presented to me only the back of her head, though she herself did not shift at all, occupied as she was with the intense focus needed to gauge her exact angle of incidence with the newly defined ground of the state we found ourselves in, until enlightenment slowly dawned on me and I traced in the set of my limbs and the vague dazzlement that spread from my brain to my eyes, the speed with which the scenery scrambled over itself around her, rendering her utter immobility vertiginously dynamic, an engine from which brimmed over the waves of heat shimmer that lapped against the gaudy effusion of azaleas and the bland realism of the blond cinderblock strip mall which together framed what was otherwise the unlimited extensibility of this panorama, so that the paucity and infrequency of any sense on my part that we had established contact, as I orbited her more and more frantically, was weighted toward the plenitude of a secret knowledge which I had to assume, in the sheer knowingness of posture with which the matte and shapeless fall of her hair proposed itself as the face to which I must address myself, that we shared between us, all my efforts at articulating my path from the point at which she had slipped beneath the reflective surface of a small volume of still water to the spot on which I presently stood being only the ongoing construction of a series of double mirrors, like those installed around the chairs at the beauty college, in which to see from all angles the receding backs of those whose close and fine-grained sharing in the texture of our bodies must take in every instance the form of a protracted departure.

"I remember having left you a promise or invitation in a jar," she mumbled, sweet and sorrowful, though still preoccupied with the acrid plane of parking slowly coagulating beneath her feet, "and it has irradiated every zone in the city, spilling over the limits of rational planning and speculative excess alike, until our faces are burned violet with its heat, about which you'll simply have to take my word, my sundial stance here having externalized your watery involutions and eddies of guilty bad faith into the unavailability of a face by which to make of me the cult statue around which your architectures would unfold. That silly playlet you scribbled on the back of the label you peeled from the keepsake vessel of my elixir was a better start, crowding your blockaded solipsism out into a domestic world dense with compacted scale and admitting your participatory joy in the path I followed toward asphyxia at the bottom of hydraulic infrastructures, as *your love tends to the complete assimilation of a person, and none is comestible by way of conversation alone.* This was the full meaning of my invitation to "shake on it," you know — that a simple injunction like "don't drink the water" was doomed in advance to fail, and that instead my wish as I faded over your horizon was that you titrate me into the medium sustaining the whole series of subsequent relations so finely that the wastewater treatment plants would fail in their stated goal of filtration, passing me along into the irrigation systems and civic fountains that swirl together in irresolvable turbulence your limited concepts of basis and decoration, until I have become the self-valorizing echo of the pleasure you take in your own refined perceptions, broadcasting back to you on all channels the great wealth of limits in which you have encased yourself, clothing your body in restriction in order to know it by the texture of a fabric it strains and bulges against."

    I began to dance with even greater haste around this effigy of my Auntie Terrible, as if to blur my revolutions of failure to connect into a solid state of present loss that would find itself sufficient to more than the terms of this single lingering subtraction from my world, for I knew that if this one undigested death had stopped me in my tracks, or rather, had assigned me to my tracks as a set of stops, a keyed melody that I followed throughout what I had approached as uniquely my composition, then the reality of hundreds, thousands, even millions of deaths burrowing into the land itself, installing themselves in the history of the cotton clothing that stuck damply to my armpits and crotch, would overwhelm not only me but the sound made by the very possibility of a city still refusing to fade entirely over the low-density horizon, and as I danced I felt the denizens of the lawn chairs dancing with me, revolving in full circle around nothing but my back as I revolved around my revenant aunt, gathered close round me in their cutoff denim shorts and sleeveless concert tees, with only the air to separate us in a mobile approximation of a carefully artless, wild-seeming but well-maintained garden, and all of us centered in the gravity of that one impossibly agile static form that would refuse for all time to be the ghost in our machine, insisting instead on remaining the machine in our ghostliness, the contraption of creaking ropes and platforms by which we descended to the staging of our inescapable sociability, or ascended unsteadily towards its heaven. Perhaps this inadvertent attraction was what allowed Auntie Terrible to slip out of the story altogether, trying on characters as one tries on clothes in thrift stores, quickly and with a sensuous indifference to fit, the richness of this scarcity becoming a rationed life that overflowed all bounds of the single body's vitality, allowing those of us who danced in turn to find ourselves a small band of armed rebels scattering through an empty city, or a series of distant siblings writing fond and bitchy letters back and forth across uncharted territories, or an alien invasion reshaping earthly life into its perfect and therefore perfectly inverted mirror image. Our pleasure in her difficult company and its capacity for repetition beyond its proper time changed us into ourselves, and then precipitated myself from this mass, the form of my new citizenship a piezoelectric crystal crackling with static through which her voice rose, stopping the dance in mid-step as she commanded me to shut up and lift her a beer from the minimart that anchored the low block building.

With the clerk stoned and watching TV, it was easy enough to steal a bottle from the cooler and return to the parking lot, passing it through the uninterrupted barrier of her hair, into which it disappeared to an echoing chorus of exaggerated swallowing sounds, as if her internal organs had been outfitted with public address speakers, this impression of the porosity between her organic functions and the dumb factuality of the place she stood being reinforced by the failure of the foamy amber liquid to disappear into an interior, her hair growing dark with wetness and then dripping onto the hot asphalt where I knelt to catch it on my outstretched tongue, hoping at last to catch the irreversible contagion of my adulthood, that amphibious afterlife of experience, from this drink we in some sense shared, and believing it the next best thing to a kiss as its icy tongue licked its way around my stomach and I puked onto my shoes.

Pacing It Off

Dear E.,

To have carried, up to this point, the account of what the narrative of these events must have been, under the sign of a lyric citationality, must be a means by which we unwittingly signal how impure our commitment to the account itself must have been from its outset — how much it owes, off the books, to the suspension of recognition enacted by our lyric proclivities, a blank check removed from commerce as a kind of negative confession. I would like to mark out from this site and what constitutes perhaps its bad faith, a direction that counterposes to the little man of letters' insistence on narrative as the necessary ground on which our present will have to come to produce its reflexive self-awareness, an approach to this particular narrative or exchange of letters that recognizes the insane lure of such self-presentation while not allowing its constitutive moments of non-equivalence to simply sluice away as the ore of experience is progressively refined for metallic circulation, into *a physical ideal of beauty which we recognize in every passing bright layer of the sun's false architecture far enough away and sufficiently opaque for its indistinct features not to belie the identification.* Or, to come around the back way, if place in the lyric is the tent or hut on the verge of being scraped off the land, and in narrative the labyrinthine passage through a plot of woods or a city, than what I'm most intrigued by in both is the possibility of holding ground against the enclosure that would retroactively naturalize such volumes and planes in the register of property — which may at least rise to the level of efficacy in dancing about agriculture, or shopping for bargain universes in a gutter. This, as you might guess, is more slippery for me than any formal commitment to the delay or ventilation of textual closure, and so I have preferred the term "enclosure" for the gesture it makes of placing these formal questions on the scale of political economy's structural violence, leaving us choking on the excess of vacancy and hearing voices that always seem to go before a scripted grand entrance whose arrival is obscured in a drift of gray powder from the air.

I suppose this brings me to my minimum definition of what such a narrative might be: a verbal sequence whose temporality is placed in relation to the time-scale of some other sequence (of unseen events that structure the experience of a vanished plot of woods, for example), such that this relation is a problem, a rhythmic wheezing between metal scaffolding and dead signals in which *there must be some sense of proportion.* Of course, as persistent as the problem itself are the evasive protocols for shunting it into a premature resolution, or sidestepping it altogether, as one allows the deafening noise of the helicopter blades to fade back into the encompassing buzz of mosquitoes and that into the vague sticky pause in which one remembers the texture of summer as if through a coarse aluminum screen. Thus on the one hand we find the well-worn but seemingly inescapable appeal to "realism" as the mode in which narrative, and specifically narrative in the novel, will align itself with social-historical time, in which our present quandary will no longer matter, being clear, while on the other hand there is the easy "experimentalism" that would collapse narrative into a one-dimensional semiosis, *a profile of today having nothing definitive about it, only a momentary resemblance to some deceased member of the family to whom nature has paid this commemorative courtesy,* perfectly iterable, unlimited but in the bad infinity's sense of dumbly literal addition, which is a somewhat updated version of what Williams was already excoriating as an "easy lateral sliding," and which elides any engagement with the time-problem at all by placing the language of the composition in a purely literary vacuole, sealed off from the world and its combative temporalities.

    Put another way, I might say that we're looking for a version of the story that acknowledges the mechanism that produces versions, a narrative that admits its uncanny double, an absence multiplying into a crowd or some note missing from our speech which introduces a sharp-edged gap in the timbre of our voices, this frequency-clipping smashing the ground of its own perception into decorative shards that assail us with everything we do not contain, *a fake series of chance encounters,* transmitted on all frequencies:

TRANSMISSION:
    inside
    in sleep
    in the way   on the path through
                        the forest in the shape
                        of quilted surfaces

                filtering a view through intervening thin clouds. Worn out by the many present suffering their consumption. They are carted away, and harmless. New urban form takes shape in languid, deadly boredom of the dense provincial patchwork carpet
                      more often than imagination
                      sees its "nowadays" as product,

                Byzantine deductions from
                an imperceptible thread,

> precious, woven tropes to
> remotest of affinities.

"He would often use a bearing wall to center
this untoward outgrowth of someone else."

Extruded slapstick at high pressure
is any body's commonplace disclosure,

and further on the work will
find the law explaining all
thereby becoming property
without examining the same.

Generally, the contract spells contraction, as the concert would spell concretion, if it ever came off. Some other States notice of non-payment immediately manufactures secrecy between the tender cogs. Thus your every excursion carries back the news before it has its satisfaction of gregarious encounters in the dark,

> apt insect grown brilliant
> destroying to protect the limbs of the

apple over the orchard, saving the readily seen scale. Maybe the mirror in some cases does become simple, so long as last resort is only in those limbs *themselves*.

But imagine yourself into this position, as if you were writing to some anonym to tell it how much you regretted its absence, and that pleasure in this respect could be like photography, your superior grasp of the narrative occupation of an empty city which you still try to produce in a dream pulling us inexorably forward through a space however blank that becomes landscape and takes on value as we progress. The dead center of that field of vision *must be well-informed about all that goes on* without it, but the tempo of walking is at no point exactly equal to the tempo of value, the less so as the landscape itself grows more and more saturated with capital and begins to pass through circuits that overlap but do no coincide with our own.

Not yours,
T.

And What We Lived For

Around every corner is another corner. A shrieking disconnect signal. Thus we maintain contact. The radio carries news of skirmishes in other quarters. I am cornered. The marvelous fountain in the bank plaza helps to keep this impression disconnected from my skin. There is only one reason why the little band and I go on missing each other in our echolocation. We miss the point. Word of them is on the radio. It is radio, cold on my skin. The word in the air is water rationing, but it is mid-day and the fountain flows. A deeded unit of moisture in a dehydrated city. A little band has left its wooded plot. They flow around corners. Green-dyed water falls toward the basin. It refracts them. Misdirects me. Once again I miss them. I miss them.

Helicopters and static have resolved any issue of friendship. The broadcast says, "This is the form in which your citizenship emerges." It was what I thought. We were all thinking the same.

Forward of that the landscape is leveled. Fundamentally, the city is flat. Is a fundamentalist city. Says the broadcast: *"The images which it brings back, far from being those of a particular face, present rather the joyless universality of a skeleton."* Forward of that, it says: "Precious froth." And: "Don't drink the water." Understand that the city is not empty. It is vacancy in excess. We are the only ones left because we are the only ones who have left. Or I am, as the skirmishes carry on around corners. Fountains fall in rich arcs. This is why the radio broadcasts our thoughts: we are all thinking the same. "I have left. I have left you there." Out of this crowd a motorcycle on its back wheel, bright flash. Crash. The fountain is empty enough to absorb the impact. Tiny circles, a few more damp spots on asphalt. Oil and water.

On this day when the light had, so to speak, destroyed reality, reality concentrated itself in certain dusky and transparent creatures which, by contrast, gave a more striking, a closer impression of life: the shadows. Full in the eyes. Angelic.

The broadcast says we'll play together in the dirt. Which is trucked in. Inescapable appeal of the ragged. The hinterlands have written this place a blank check. It is wealth, nowhere to be found. The fountain. The foundation. *At once overdressed and half naked.* An exception to the genitality of persons you thought. I thought the same. I have stolen a new green shirt from a cracked display window and am awaiting orders. Have made the facts a problem. Life here is really pretty uneventful. Pleasant, even. There is light here and food for the taking. Around the corner, screaming. Which is canned soup, escaping the ragged edges of a can behind a display window. Explosive decompression. Faces of command refract brightly in the shards. Alone among them, I march in formation. Faces of comrades, aunts, terrible memories. *And friendship is not merely devoid of virtue, like conversation, it is fatal to us as well.* "You know you're impossible," says the broadcast.

No discord can possibly separate me and the city. I am myself, and I am still it. This I will say on the radio when I reach my comrades, who have taken the broadcast tower. Great wealth, it will turn the planes of streets into nature. Green will be my uniform: stolen shirt, treated water, cracked paint on a motorcycle leaking oil. Self-valorizing value, chafed and sore hands.

I sing along with the radio. Lip-synch with the face on the high glass screens that shatter. Distribute their wealth invisibly throughout the city. Decoration eating into the brushed concrete surfaces. Exotic complication, and then return. The returns. The refrain: "In this way, with a summary to refer to, you know where you are."

But the summary remains. Public address pukes dumb factuality. Remains, at the start as at the finish. Skidding across hot asphalt, I cannot disappear into an interior. I am remains. The notebook says so, in sum. It is here, washed into the gutter from the distant woods. I have wrecked my stolen bike. Fetched up against a high curb. It is what is left. *A zone of interchangeable charms.* Spelling it out, I add remains to the body of my work. To what remains of my body, shattered in the wreck.

At last, I have found a friend. Long hair slick with motor oil. Leathery, emaciated. She cracks a finger, then another. The hand prepares to reach into daylight. It seizes my notebook. "This is a blueprint," she says, "for wreckage. I will write our names in it." Fundamentally, everything travels away from here. Her hand passes over me. It is independent of both of us. A dog eats from the gutter. Someone's foot, maybe mine. "Your capacity for repetition," she says. And: "Shut up." She reads: "Location scouting." And: "Soundtrack. Shot list." Her voice rises, crackling. She rises to go. Bites my hand, it stings. Swells. There will be no snatching the notebook away from her now. I am obliged to laugh. A leathery crackle, skin breaks. The dog sniffs the air. Remains unmoved.

"This is real empathy," I say. I am not used to speaking here, and it is loud. Echoes. I turn away from what recreates my voice. "Real empathy," the city spits up. "Our destroyed bodies reappear to each other. And you put yourself inside my skin. Others call this stabbing, slashing." Even the vein dissembles. Pulses to a rhythm neither hers nor mine. A lapse into the second person, from either side. Now everything knows where we are. We are remaining here. *We wish to remain, for the one we love, the unknown person whom she may love in turn.* The inadvertent attraction of overflow. Trash and meat clog the fountains. A wreck. Flooded streets, a perfectly inverted mirror.

"You look how your notebook sounds," she says. "Blank repletion." She slips beneath the surface of the water. Becomes all reflection. Becomes the city. A line inscribed around the infinite. Thus my territorial definitions. Thus the antidote to fire in the wooded plot. A gaudy effusion of masonry. Protracted departure into our ability to remain together. The waves brim over. I slip beneath. They slap at me, repeating. The rhythm of the notebook. Our skins sting.

If the city slips beneath the waves, everything will reflect there. A single lingering subtraction. Sound that would refuse to fade. We maintain this water garden. Gather the remains away from it. Pile them up, dirt and sharp rocks. Piled on our fragile eyes. Remains of everything but the city. Now we have this machine. We can begin. We can echo. "I will take you to her," says my friend, aspirating water. Our aspiration is reflected from the tower. Alone above the water, it reflects the land itself. Which is nowhere, submerged. The dogs dig into the earth piled on our eyes. "I will take you to her," I say. I do not see her. My eyes are crushed by the remains. The face, unavailable, is the promise of a city. An invitation to begin. We have known this all our lives. Which is to say, not at all. Slowly, the flood coagulates. Watery involutions become architecture.

Carried on the swell, we rise to the tower. Not much remains. The horizon has risen. The tower is a hut. The rest of the city swirls as a fountain. "What's new?" I ask of the absent face reflected in the glass there. And: "Are there dry clothes?" "Don't drink the water," a self-valorizing echo at the limits of broadcast, comes as no answer. I pretend not to care. Curbed by wet denim in dark green. This is where we live, it is always starting like this.

We Would Shake Hands

... in a straightforward, friendly sort of way, like good pals, but there was never a word said about kissing, and yet we weren't any the less friends for that.

The television would always flicker on across the room at such moments. In our horror of turning to face it, we would flick our eyes along the wall until we found them brought up short in a glass that safely reversed the import of whatever message we otherwise might have received. At such moments a radar scan flickered in the mirror.

MIRROR:

>Notation's *I*, on stage,
>leaves the low last
>threnody supposed
>>as chosen.

>Besides, these works
>of dubious transmission

>trouble one. "Cut!
>Because of him, of her, I play
>the test tone as another friend to cheater and to thief."

>>Sit down, sit down and function!
>>And know I speak the truth:

>Money praises
>critical instruction.

>>You have my gorge of color, glut
>>of faint untouching to unthread
>>>and make cohere again.

Each unit cuts the angle down,
the incline following along the way
the grain lies down in cultivated voice.
Whether it's a drag or not, the figure
is her own slow labor to identify:

Constructed flame
And crushing trifles

Narrative Occupation and Uneven Enclosure

Dear T.,

So the letter finally gets where it was going all along, a foreign body isolated in a strange environment with which it is nonetheless isomorphic, and you can insert here (I'll leave a blank) your picture of one of Terry Riley's early experiments with multiple tape loops of various lengths running from a spindle out into every corner of the studio, and often out windows onto the surrounding grounds, collecting bits of dirt and dust on the way, or you can find another place to put your elaborate apologia, having forgotten me entirely in order to get me into the story in the first place. What I think you might have been reaching for, in the fancy-dress occasion that replaced the threat I posed to you but managed still to register a few moments during which the flesh was evident behind the rich brocade or tattered poly-cotton blend and in which we rediscovered features of a body that was intimately yours or mine not despite, but because of the great duration of its passage through other hands, startled by its alien self-similarity, was a disposition of narrative that addresses our experience riven between two or more time-space scales, in the sense of knowing that to elaborate a track across this landscape is ultimately to impoverish or underdevelop some constituent of the vectoral multiplicity of possible developments it initially poses. So, a going forward while knowing that one has to go back, and knowing that going back remains a kind of forward motion that will not fully recover the initial lapse, playing both sides against a middle where any thought of territory undoes itself through the force of its own capacity to replace whatever you might have been thinking of it with a forced decision that is not unlike love, or sleep. In this sense the contradictory nature of experience is not only translated back and forth between us into sequence, but more strongly traduced, by a method which pushes its infidelities to the forefront at every opportunity, our spasms of pleasure on repeatedly taking leave of each other vanishing so deeply into our interiors that we become interchangeable with the velocity of change in the neighborhood of our exchange.

But these are the shapeless fragments, capable of reconstitution, of that thought which you have caused to explode, by striking it against the will of some other, indifferent as to whom, this vagueness in fact creating a welcoming alcove into which I can reassert my presence here despite your attempts to drown or allegorize me out of the picture, and thus exploit the capacity of these fragments to become lost or confused in a kind of second-order fragmentation after a certain quantitative length is reached in their intricate grammatical subordination, an interval of perhaps a single letter across which appearance fails to shake hands with the guarantee of reappearance. (I should mention that I first noted the dynamic I'm proposing here in the standard English translation of Proust, so thanks are due to Moncrieff and Kilmartin for their inadvertent contribution, as to you for rebroadcasting what's on my mind in the form of heaps of old tires and televisions that are your best approach to a limited specificity). The lack of declension in what we write to one another allows sentences of an arbitrarily long extension to "forget themselves," so that even in a sentence where later parsing reveals a normative construction, the reader (one of us, passing notes through the woods) experiences modifiers sliding away from nouns and verbs, multiply-embedded subordinate clauses breaking their subordination to the main clause, erotic dreams abandoning their object under canvas dropcloths and tattered survey markers, etc., in short, a world that falls far short of filling us up individually, and isn't even up to the attempt to color in the civic earth that articulates our separation. The total effect is one of forward motion that continually falls back upon itself, maximal fullness of syntactical elaboration becoming an odd kind of lack, as if the world were to eject us in order to form itself in the image of our voices, where we might "return to ourselves" in the story of a plot of woods that was or was not destroyed with us or within us or nowhere near us, the whole tangle reaching into daylight with a kind of damp attentiveness to the city of its presumed exile.

Or you could mark out an entirely different approach to the problem, through the paragraph or block of prose by way of Stein's oft-repeated maxim that paragraphs are emotional while sentences are not, positing time as primarily an emotional category, and building a forward narrative motion most often achieved in the movement from paragraph to paragraph, while the individual sentences that make up a paragraph display a hovering sort of relation to each other, the capacity for repetition taking the place of the single, fatal phrase, as in the following, which has been my point exactly, all along:

> The summary remains. Public address pukes dumb factuality. Remains, at the start as at the finish. Skidding across hot asphalt, I cannot disappear into an interior. I am remains. The notebook says so, in sum. It is here, washed into the gutter from the distant woods. I have wrecked my stolen bike. Fetched up against a high curb. It is what is left. *A zone of interchangeable charms.* Spelling it out, I add remains to the body of my work. To what remains of my body, shattered in the wreck.
>
> At last, I have found a friend. Long hair slick with motor oil. Leathery, emaciated. She cracks a finger, then another. The hand prepares to reach into daylight. It seizes my notebook. "This is a blueprint," she says, "for wreckage. I will write our names in it."

I need to insist that the preposition in that final sentence is crucial: your name and mine are *in* that notebook, not *on* it, as we turn our faces from each other into the accidents that mar what we had hoped to transmit, and, impossible as it sounds, find that the whole episode of fire, wandering, occupation and breakdown was written to include us in its unfoldings, so that what we have amused ourselves with in these letters emerges as the residual, consolatory fiction it is, a screen however large and glassy in its civic dimensions and capacity to address us from the highest towers, which is at bottom only our aversion to understanding that all the numbing repetition we approached as interlinear commentary to our "real work" of correspondence was actually a precise present-tense account of the state we found ourselves in, as we find ourselves faced with the colossal task of unpacking a city from a half-submerged hut.

In the suburb, where this work begins for us, serial iteration is the modality of the domestic and civic spaces of bodily experience, and thus death finally assumes its historical vocation of complete obscenity, wandering entirely offstage. This is not to say that the suburb conquers death or finds a bypass loop around enclosure, but that death here becomes the assumed prerequisite, that which is understood as necessarily taken care of elsewhere: infrastructure. The bypass loop is there, a constituent support of the neighborhood, occupying our bodies beneath our attention, like a soul.

As it happens, the time of this groundskeeping labor coincides with a period in which the rolling wave of accumulation crises dating, for the sake of convenience, to 1974, begin to exert an exaggerated pressure on real estate, and the intensification of relations between social landscape and speculative capital become, for a certain class and region, a matter of direct experience, culminating logically, and originating experientially, with a series of police raids on escheat zoning plats on the exurban fringe, which have until now been squatted by homeless families and used for various illicit pleasures and conflicts by young people housed in the surrounding low-rent neighborhoods. The time in which we set about periphrastically narrating this overlap of times overlaps itself with the intensification of several other modes of land occupation on a more global scale: the IDF incursions into Gaza and the West Bank, along with the construction of the "separation barrier," speculation in terrestrial resources along the lines of Bechtel's water privatization scheme in Bolivia, and the preparation, execution and disaster of the U.S.-British imperialist adventure in Iraq, so that, if one were to trace a rhythm of experience across the surfaces of a place, one would have to come to terms in some fashion with the displacements of a series, variously motivated, variously consequential, and elaborated along widely divergent lines, of what have come to seem geopolitical enclosures acts. While these enclosures stem from an emergent global order, I will insist, despite my uncertain status and near-total absence from the narratives built around me, on highlighting the unevenness of their mutual relations in time and space, locating for you (since you refuse to do it for yourself) the incommensurabilities in the proposed myth of a total system in which resistances might be imagined.

You wait, hoping that I didn't mean it, and that I will return to send your hope scattering with a quick flick of the light switch, scattering petals of light across the indoor-outdoor carpet for you to trample with your bare feet. Around this corner, I might find a place to which your voice will not carry, in which I will be the figure of transmission around which you've been circling:

RADIO *[out to pasture in the center of the earth]*:
    First turn to have the eyes,
    know the gardens in each season.
    "I'm security." "I'm a vegetable, a sap.
    Call me contact poison."

  He was plenty of ground between themselves—and plenty of profile offered like a broad expanse of back, though his attacker was none nearby. Resisters flee into the forest still, deeper into every bush in the park.

> Kept the entity from engulfing the arrow, the nickname from overwhelming praxis, tender and talked-to. Row by row the profit of them, while the bodies stayed with mother. Believe or don't believe she knew, but she wanted (also felt guilty about) the other recovering children.

> > And yet, presence to delight,
> > people to disturb, harassed
> > slight contrast in the plural of
> > his tiny body.

From here, I shall no longer have to overhear as you find occasion through your complicit hesitations *to have others play to you that music the voiceless rendering of which does not suffice you,* letting the nametags drop with a percussive rhythmic click into the desk drawer, to be retrieved casually by the surveillance robots as they scour the house in a frozen or submerged interval, setting the stage for the next moment with nothing to disturb the succession, except that someone will be saying my name, for whatever reason.

Always,
A.T.

The Reader,
or, Skin Flicks I Remember

…caught in which of the infallible fulcrums turned into a gill-set hook? Also sprung holes in the hardwood striped with strong figures of an absent face. The horns of a prisoner's dilemma pulled soft as taffy, sticking in the damp hair. Nylon webbing fastened to the deck chairs. Picture frames on hard diagonal skew prevent the portrait's lipid warp.

Clinch: to bend the light. Smothered behind the door. For latch, read "tongue adhering to the salt along one face." But the transmitting mechanism is as often mounted flush on an interior wall.

In the Rearview Hindsight Is Dead Ahead

Someone will be saying my name, for whatever reason, and being thus called from within the interstices of the scene itself, I will find myself caught in the collapse of distinction between within and without, and forced back into attendance on a subsidized solipsism *whose principal charm is that it is silhouetted against the sea.*

Even now I sit alone at the kitchen table, pinching the tops of my ears for hours at a time, hoping to crush the cartilage down to a point, to resemble some elf or gnome on a fantasy calendar with which I found myself infatuated as a child and to which I have maintained this odd relation only because the unlikeliness of that airbrushed figure places it at equal removes of unlikeness from all three or more versions of what has happened to put me in the place where I live, making of it a switching substation like the humming nest of galvanized steel and aluminum on the far side of the drainage culvert, which my slow-moving curiosity only this afternoon has finally discovered as the reason for the filled-in and non-resonating spaces in the neighborhood's air, though I would seem to an observer intent even now on ascribing the phenomenon to some character out of nineteenth-century lumpen melodrama, or to our continued tenancy in the decrepit duplex of which I cannot help but imagine anyone both landlord and aggrieved evictee in serial iteration of the only two available positions, hoping to exhaust the structure itself and experience death onstage. Thus neatly I divide the landscape between fantasy and poured concrete, *dazzled with the stupendous revelation that I exist in someone's mind,* in this harsh glare falling constantly down the storm sewers and drowning by proxy in bathtubs, and in this rapid superimposition the mirror shows a kind of undertone, or five o'clock shadow in entirely the wrong color, marking in uneven blotches the nodes at which my face inflects toward a second, a third, a fourth, fluid and vague as a shifting light trampled underfoot. I have a flattering picture of myself as a carpenter, an open-ended analogy if ever there was one, though based loosely on what you might call biography, which is itself the arrow of an index for a trained internalized assistant, a bare idea of collective life, holding up an apple, plus the row of shelves lined with faded snapshots of the elaborate preparations leading up to each and every likewise failed trick through which I sleep at such high velocity that I have remained, for all this time, just outside the moment of waking, assuming the bypass loop in the infrastructure of a beauty that remains a problem for existence, and which satisfies the onlooker by becoming ugly, if larger, up close.

REAL ESTATE CHANNEL:
From a hill one passes to a grotto, a meadow, rocks, a stream, a pit, another hill, a marsh, but knows that they are there only to enable the hippopotamus,

zebra, crocodile, albino rabbit, bear and heron to disport themselves in a natural or picturesque setting, and to give the Buddy Nation, Inc. Fantastic Robot Landscape Grounds Crew and Menagerie Management Team something to which they might apply themselves, an emergent global order highlighting the unevenness of the lawn, while they wait around to say the magic words that get the television working once again.

Through the moiré patterns of multiple interposed chain-link fences, it's impossible for me to tell whether you are dancing or standing in line for emergency supplies — it's the effect you buy, not the carton you are busy tearing your way into, which is most useful as a medium for the flow of a regressive tax — but either way I am filled with you, occupied as a body by a soul, or the neighborhood by a newly widened and regraded roadway, and I know that you are there because you dig me out of the collapsed lean-to by which I hoped to have effected a change of address without getting out of bed, and your trowels have drawn a bit of blood without managing yet to make a sound, given that *what is lacking here is the means of commotion.* High society is indeed riding the bus, licking its lips, talking into thin air about an actor who, looking unremarkable enough, carries in his wake something that burns through film stock as the intensification of the modes of occupation. *In the intervals between the blare of the instruments, at high tide, in the gliding surge of a wave heard again and again, slurred and continuous, seeming to enfold these notes in its crystal spirals and to be spraying its foam over the intermittent echoes of a submarine music,* through the heavy curtains of our direct experience of real estate, can you come out and play?

Free, With Serial Reservations

RADIO:
[voiceover] ...that those features represent categories.

[location report]
Channel muck turned topsoil in the park. Called treads, they are not feet.
Pure domination opens up its metrics...general admission...
       to a fault, free sulfur hiss each word — give it away
      surplus or a slip   between the ribs, no joke
  airs out around her in circumferential turning
radio dial   projectile teenage polity   "independence"
— or the coast   downslope of bridge to the city burning fumes
more *sense* on sordid work release, exempt. Prisons on the map in red
       stamp you with the ring of self-address. Or the cost.
When threat bulletins   tunnel crossfade   *other voices cancel*
  the result   bug-sized   still a force, broken skin across the issue
              in notation, temperament made music
   overcrowding — buses for the field trip offscreen, a modern reclamation
            bringing in the new subscriber base.
    And recall those instruments work the grade on curves,
   bees — to nest in yellow insulation overspill
         from this vaunting of your ear: your car.
     Relocate *that* survival from the fields and shops of process
every gauge, every bit of copper wire stripped for salvage
            ran the calculation hard before design
            started something incomplete as
  ...that sand erased the only highway, I said goodbye my love
with brick placed under tongue, men and women still themselves
            into inertia, their tremendous need.

That it move from hand to mouth direct   a lemon, is the problem
I revert to   unproductive curbside slush   civilized
            with short-haul freight: sewer sludge, cable spools
    rewind the measure of that distance, fooled by the orbiting cut.
No hope for bodies — is excess mass, poured into the pylons
            that image bring wildness, bring a rage
            to grief at the blunt end of the wedge —

            broadcast gravity, head pulled away from skull
                    forward of continuous English
        and the body greased for passage down the pipe.
            Shape is the new emptiness, proposes this
country to a product listing   listening   to all
the pyramid display of unit-valued sovereignty. Cheap imported citrus
        in your saliva ends up trickling down my throat.
Here is the cascade of mending, perfection of hydraulic needs
complex geometry for occupants marched cell to cell
                    closed by force
        the ranks of track lighting, bruised air.
Whence the vision: here will I love you   through the grate
                — reveals the mirror
    at least, as burial in view to stand its ground

                mounded up against the k-rails.
        Staring at the legs, willing them to walk
                the well-paved or well-built
self-similar Romanesque   either iteration   or the dome offset
to follow camp through pores of landscape
            in the lonely instance, escaping past the lip.

OCCUPANT:

I'm not sure what day it is. I think we danced together for quite a while, perhaps more than one night. I can hardly move my limbs. In the end, he gave my hand a straightforward, friendly shake and I sent him home. Most likely, I was so surprised to discover my features intact after the Replacement Protocol had run its course that I fell back on this most conventional of behaviors for reassurance. I'm struck even now by how many of these still-intact features are things I hadn't noticed in years, but that seem now to have been waiting for my reacquaintance, despite my lack of any expectation of finding them again. The crooked little toe on my right foot, broken in a baseball game when I was fourteen. The puckered dark mole midway up my left forearm. Things like that. If I have been replaced, it's an excellent job they've done. Meanwhile, I have discarded the ICR, since all channels seem to be crowded with the single feature of myself that spread through the central transmitters as I danced and broadcast in my trance state. I don't need to hear that anymore. I'm not sure that you do, either, except I'm less sure of there being a "you" to address this to. And I think the startling self-similarity I've recovered in myself might look entirely different, were I to find you again.

Oh, but you should have seen the clear spasm of pleasure that ran from his stomach up through his shoulders and suffused his face when I shook his hand and released him! He practically *floated* away over the asphalt, which was already growing hot in the ten o'clock sun. The last I saw, he had stolen a too-small bike left behind by one of the analogues, and was pedaling around the corner. His vanishing was not so much into the distance as into an interior, and his charms have become interchangeable with the unchanged but wholly different landscape of the neighborhood. It was as if he had seen exactly what was on my mind and had left me to it. Talking into the azalea bushes that mark the line between the Place and the wooded plot behind it, I feel as if I'm talking to him still. And given what I experienced of Warbler sensitivity to communication, I have a hunch I might be speaking for a more general audience as well. Certainly I don't feel the loss of my transmission and recording gear: the branches of the older oaks visible through the hedge, the clumps of palmetto, the piles of neighborhood junk abandoned in the clearings — old tires, rusted box springs, smashed television sets — seem to shimmer at their edges in time with my speech. I know I am being recorded and rebroadcast, even though they have come to the end of my immediate usefulness and left me behind. This is where I live now, or am starting to.

For the past few nights I have camped in the dumpster, unsure whether to return to a world that ejected me in order to form itself in the image of my voice, or draw up my own blueprint for a country that will surely end up in wreckage. My most recent attempt at this was unsatisfying. As the Warbler command override faded from my body, still half in a trance, I dictated to my dancing partner the events of the mission that had brought me to meet him here. After his departure, I found his notebook, dropped in the gutter in front of the minimart. His transcription had turned our encounter into a savage little parlor drama, set in a bathroom, into which the voices of an ambiguous commerce filtered to shape the action, such as it was. I recognized the broad contours of our encounter in it, but still, I can't believe that it was my condition alone that was responsible for the deformations of shape imposed upon it. I have preferred to leave the rest of it unread, lest I conclude that the attentiveness of his damp and sympathetic brown eyes obscured a reserve of contempt. The notebook is buried at the back of the dumpster, under a discarded barbecue grill, if anyone should decide to look for it.

Meanwhile the forest stretches more and more confidently through the hedge, a hand reaching into daylight. Perhaps it is not too soon to speak of the question of inhabitants, clustered back there around what I imagine to be a shallow pond, still as cypress knees, *motionless lightfoot guardians darkening the water's surface with their viscous bodies and the attentive gaze of their deep blue eyes.* Maybe it's only a nesting owl, or the remnants of the herds of wild swine that once tilled every inch of this ground, pulling up the roots. Fundamentally, everything travels away from here. At last, I have found my footing. I have no desire for more duets, dramatic pairings beset by externalities of judgment as if we were figure skaters. Alright, even now it seems a stray transmission finds its way home. But the televisions only a step or two from here are irreversibly shattered. The point remains: I was promised a city. I will turn my face away from you (or your residual fiction, if I must address some second person) and build it myself out of the involutions of water in the pond I have assigned to a place I haven't visited yet. I will make the pond, too, if that's what's needed. The accidents that mar the transmission you have become in full will become a substitute for electricity, powering my construction project. They will light the beacons I will place to draw others to my cause. *You can come and sit by my bed and watch me eat, if you like, and afterwards we'll play at anything that you choose.* But I know you, even replaced in full as you have been, I sniff the air like a dog and feel you there, not heading this way just yet, but soon. And I know that you will snatch this back from me into the notebook. I should not have told you where I hid it. My capacity for repetition ran that fatal phrase too long.

But I will dig into the earth, somewhere, and start again. That pile of dirt and sharp rocks, simple shelter and repurposed remains will be my city. I will continue to file reports — I remain your humble, etc., plus I can't shake the work ethic you slipped into my cell memory — but lingering there will crush your eyes from the scene. I have this work to do, machines to build from canvas dropcloths, tattered survey markers, jagged squares of corrugated tin. None of this will have been replaced, and so you'll find no place in it. *How could this world have lasted longer than myself, since I am not lost in its vastness, since it is the world that is enclosed in me, in me whom it falls far short of filling, in me who, feeling that there is room to store so many other treasures, fling the dumpster, the hydraulic chairs, the pawned jewelry and guns, the refrigerated inventory contemptuously into a corner?*

This is real empathy. I am putting myself inside your skin. Like scabies. There's an interval — call it a single letter, if we're to translate it into alphabetic terms for easy comprehension — between your appearance and your reappearance. I live there. *We* live there, and plan on remaining. I'm sure there are others, there must be. I'm scrawling a banner in charcoal from the discarded grill, and we'll cohere under that.

Your antidote to this, recreated now as its own replacement, is all reflection. What I mean is that you think you're playing both sides against a middle that simply slips out of your territorial definitions. Because of your territorial definitions, which are your love for the world. Which brings me to my decision, finally: I need a place to sleep. *I will dwell in you like one of those foreign bodies which it would be wiser when all is said to expel, but which you leave where they are without disturbing them, so harmless for the present does their weakness, their isolation amid a strange environment render them.* This is a mistake you can't help but make. Given that this gap is where I will remain, I have decided on a place that doesn't smell so much like trash and rancid meat glued together with spoiled milk and hair cuttings swept out with the dust. Besides, the lack of density out here in the open renders me conspicuous, inadvertently attractive for the purposes of your story as a kind of overflow. I will find another place.

Maybe in the woods. I can see a few tents and trailers back there.

Earlier That Same Day...

Let's try it again this way: I had come home after an evening spent in places about which I would not tell the house's other occupants, though *into my closed room they had been drifting already for hours, summoned there by my desire to see them, slipping between my thoughts and the object, whatever it might have been, upon which I was trying to concentrate them, whirling in front of me like those brown spots that sometimes, whatever we may be looking at, will seem to be dancing or swimming before our eyes,* playing in and among the intermittent echoes of a gliding surge of real estate on whose crest the oaks and cypresses are getting up and walking once again, clearing whole stretches of forest to make their point about the too much one has asked for and received, the lack of any essential solidarity between the parts of a hometown one has left, already, more than once and less than a mile down the road

"Hey, kid," they whispered, addressing themselves to *that adolescence which, while gradually dwindling until it becomes no more than a thin trickle that often runs dry, is sometimes prolonged throughout the whole course of one's life,* the calling-out of which is always a severer command than any occasion on which another simply says one's name, "with only leftovers standing, you should know what's what."

It's true, at least, that sudden bursts of white light, focused through a bit of glass high in space on unremarkably sunny days, caught and incinerated some protrusion on the palmetto-dotted plain far less often in those days, and it had been years since an armadillo died for the myth of my mobility, so long in fact, that the night before I had needed to sit down and have a good long look at some pictures, just to recall what one looked like, but still, someone kept leaving the door open, personal effects scattered all around the room among the crowd of unremarkable relatives who talked and talked into thin air, which I took as evidence of automatism on a larger scale than I could get my head around, the atmosphere as if by some internal process peeling off into layers, each of which professed to be a version of what had transpired, so that the thinness of the air was an effect not of scarcity but of multiplicity, what would have been a crowd of transmissions segregating itself among the non-integer frequencies.

DELAYED TRANSMISSION:
>contradictory at seams the swelling
armature from arms' embrace returned fire
to a cold lump of ballast the battle
so under brick tongues licking

>singing while you're at it aggression might
imply just time a stake
in the heart of the matter
of facts' ass-backward bloody drag

>*a series of interminable* terminal
states bordered in congested tissues
imply a just time's stake in
your singing at aggression while it might

>yet turn that weight to throw a bolt
into the public works away at you

    That's all so much meteorology, against which I simply hoped to appear, flatteringly backlit if that could be arranged, and *live actually in a human atmosphere,* deaf and unconcernedly adult in my slow-moving curiosity and long-term tenancy.
    I had so much skin, collapsing on me like an abandoned lean-to, but I had lost so much more. And so I was thin and grown, alone with my certainty of poured concrete divided from my architectural fantasies by a subsequent stage or two of infill, but only that wrinkled and translucent drapery of what I had shed to make myself plain to my own sight as if it were my existence in someone else's mind, were it laid out as a fine tissue from power plant to port to culvert to kumquat tree, and

threaded through the chain-link in every kind of knot one could conceive, would have been the membrane around the balloon payment, the final installment on the property. A tarp on that scale, stretched over the building materials, would have been enough to hold down the piles of fine dust and warrant what I said, and still say, often enough anyhow, not knowing what it was I had and hence ironic in default of such certainty, the magic words unlocking the whole order and leveling the unevenness of the lawn: "I know what's mine." I tried to imagine that the series of events had not yet come to this, but remained in unstable equilibrium on a pause or halt at any one of its junctures, over which my own movements had yielded only the barest brush of flesh, a hand trailing absently along a blond cinderblock wall, and that it hovered there, a ball whose bob and tumble at the peak of a water jet was held lightly by a photographic surface promising that repetition would worry at the surface of day until a spiderweb of cracks fanned out from it. Through that scrim, as the emulsion rubbed thin and flaked off, I saw the night gases rising brightly from the bay.

Atelos was founded in 1995 as a project of Hip's Road and is devoted to publishing, under the sign of poetry, writing that challenges the conventional definitions of poetry, since such definitions have tended to isolate poetry from intellectual life, arrest its development, and curtail its impact.

All the works published as part of the Atelos project are commissioned specifically for it, and each is involved in some way with crossing traditional genre boundaries, including for example, those that would separate theory from practice, poetry from prose, essay from drama, the visual image from the verbal, the literary from the non-literary, and so forth.

The Atelos project when complete will consist of 50 volumes.

The project directors and editors are Lyn Hejinian and Travis Ortiz. The director for text production and design is Travis Ortiz; the director for cover production and design is Ree Katrak.

Atelos (current volumes):

1. *The Literal World*, by Jean Day
2. *Bad History*, by Barrett Watten
3. *True*, by Rae Armantrout
4. *Pamela: A Novel*, by Pamela Lu
5. *Cable Factory 20*, by Lytle Shaw
6. *R-hu*, by Leslie Scalapino
7. *Verisimilitude*, by Hung Q. Tu
8. *Alien Tatters*, by Clark Coolidge
9. *Forthcoming*, by Jalal Toufic
10. *Gardener of Stars*, by Carla Harryman
11. *lighthouse*, by M. Mara-Ann
12. *Some Vague Wife*, by Kathy Lou Schultz
13. *The Crave*, by Kit Robinson

14. *Fashionable Noise: On Digital Poetics*, by Brian Kim Stefans
15. *Platform*, by Rodrigo Toscano
16. *Tis of Thee*, by Fanny Howe
17. *Poetical Dictionary*, Lohren Green
18. *BlipSoak01*, by Tan Lin
19. *The Up and Up*, by Ted Greenwald
20. *Noh Business*, by Murray Edmond
21. *Open Clothes*, by Steve Benson
22. *Occupational Treatment*, by Taylor Brady

Distributed by:

Small Press Distribution   Atelos
1341 Seventh Street   P. O. Box 5814
Berkeley, California   Berkeley, California
    94710-1403   94705-0814

to order from SPD call 510-524-1668 or toll-free 800-869-7553
fax orders to: 510-524-0852
order via e-mail: orders@spdbooks.org
order online: www.spdbooks.org

Occupational Treatment
was printed in an edition of 600 copies
at Thomson-Shore, Inc.
Text design and typesetting by Travis Ortiz.
Cover Design by Travis Ortiz
Cover Photograph, "Untitled" (2004) from
Hotel Series, by Melissa Dyne.